THE
NECKTIE
MAN

THE
NECKTIE
MAN

THE SENTIMENTAL JOURNEY OF A WINDRUSH TEENAGER & TRADE UNION PIONEER

Navel (Neville) Foster Clarke O.D., C.D.

PELICAN
PUBLISHERS

Kingston, Jamaica

First published in Jamaica, 2021 by Pelican Publishers

19 Balmoral Avenue,
Kingston 10, Jamaica, W.I
Tel: (876) 978-8377 Fax: (876) 978-0048
Email: info@pelicanpublishers.com
Website: www.pelicanpublishers.com

© 2021 Navel (Neville) Foster Clarke

ISBN: 978-976-8309-01-3

Cover, Book Design and Layout by Pelican Graphics

ENDORSEMENTS FOR NECKTIE MAN

The Jamaica National Group is pleased to be associated with the publication of The Necktie Man, The Sentimental Journey of a Windrush Teenager, which chronicles the life of veteran trade unionist, Navel Clarke in the United Kingdom. Like me, I believe other readers will be moved by his experience from being on board the "SS Castle Verde" to London.

We applaud Navel for taking the initiative to record his contribution to the Trade Union movement in the absence of their doing so. We believe this book will be well received by Jamaicans living in Jamaica and the Diaspora.

Hon. Earl Jarrett, OJ, CD, JP
Deputy Chairman and Chief Executive Officer
The Jamaica National Group Limited

The Windrush odyssey depicting the existential experience of life in Britain, led a young Navel Clarke to quickly conform to its hurried pace and discover for himself his true purpose in life.

His account of his experience, and rise to prominence as an advocate of the working class, spurred him, on his return to Jamaica, to continue the struggle with an intensity of desire and determination, which led him to organise Jamaica's largest white-collar union, UCASE, and demonstrated the discipline and tenacity in his advocacy, as a law maker, on behalf of the labour movement.

Danny Roberts, CD, JP
Head, Hugh Shearer Labour Studies Institute,
The UWI, Open Campus

Contents

ACKNOWLEDGEMENTS

Writing this book that recounts so much of my life was both daunting and exhilarating. It became much easier as I was surrounded by persons who celebrate me and keep me focused. As such I am truly indebted to my son-in-law Wilson, and my daughters, Anita and Paula for their staunch support.

Having completed the manuscript, I needed a publisher who would provide guidance in this my first venture and Pelican Publishers was more than able to provide the professional requirements.

I warmly acknowledge the support given by the Grace Kennedy Group in the advancement of this project and I am especially thankful to The Hon. Earl Jarrett O. J. and the JN Group for their tangible support and endorsement of the publication.

Finally, to all the persons who somehow helped me to 'write' this story by contributing to my life directly or indirectly, to include the various Trade Union organisations I have served, former employers, government officials both in Jamaica & the UK, and dear friends and family.

I thank you all.

PREFACE

Migrating to England from the Caribbean in the 1950s was perhaps not a great idea, especially for a teenager. My limited life experiences and the unknown expectations of the future created bewilderment of an unimaginable dimension.

The journey to a country so far from home, took great courage and commitment to overcome the challenges as they arose. It was indeed a challenging time. But during my journey and prolonged stay in England for twenty years, I succeeded in breaking down barriers and establishing a platform on which others of my race could build in the future.

In 1975 I decided to return to Jamaica. I truly believed that my early involvement in the trade union and political movement in England, and in particular, the borough of Brent, I would have been given the recognition that ensured my legacy from which future generations of the black working class could draw inspiration. Unfortunately, the disappointing reality that confronted me over time was, all my achievements during my twenty years in England were known only by me.

Even my friends with whom I spoke on my return visits made no reference to events political or trade union on the occasions when we met. It was as if matters of such significance in that historic period were just a fleeting illusion. My dancing skills and adolescent skirmishes were the topics that seemed worthy of remembering, hence dominated their conversations.

Eventually, this deafening silence triggered my curiosity to know how widespread this amnesia or ignorance of my work among the population, particularly in the borough of Brent, where I lived and served the people for 15 years, and the Trade Union Congress for ten years was.

On a visit to London in 1997, I made a courtesy call on a meeting of the Brent Trades Council which I headed for six years from 1969-1975. On introducing myself to the members, they were surprised to know that I was once the general secretary of the organization. Their response was that they found no record of my relationship with the Council. Further checks with the Trade Union Congress resulted in a similar response.

Having concluded that there appears to be a clear and deliberate act of erasing a black man's work and achievements from the annals of history, I made the decision to tell my story to the world in the simplest and most truthful way by writing this book. I hope you will enjoy reading. God bless us all.

The struggle continues...

PROLOGUE
THE BLACK MAN'S FINEST HOUR

The black population, specifically from the West Indies, was steadily growing in places like Brixton, Paddington and the East End of London. Jamaicans began opening clubs and cook shops, catering to our culture and cuisine. There was the Blue Orchid Club in the West End off Regent Street and the Calypso Club on Powis Terrace between Ladbrook Grove and Notting Hill. We were able to purchase, on weekends in particular, a pot of curried chicken and a pot of rice and peas from Ladbrook Grove for our parties. Liquor was rough cider and VP wines mixed, and more often than not, Teacher's Whiskey, which was purchased for fifteen shillings per bottle.

Despite all the enjoyment and the new places to go, we still had to contend with the violence of the Teddy Boys, who saw us, especially the younger blacks, as a threat. As our population grew, housing became more difficult to obtain. The older West Indians began to pool funds together in what was and perhaps still is known as a partner scheme, and thus were able to make deposits on part vacant houses. The sitting white tenants were very resentful of black people becoming owners of properties in which they were living for many years. The teenagers among them reacted violently, which was met with an equal or more vicious reaction from young and old West Indians alike. The violence escalated in the now-famous riot in and around Notting Hill Gate in August 1958 and continued into September of that year.

Even before the riot, some persons were attacked after leaving the Calypso Club, located in the North Kensington area, not far from Notting Hill itself, but unfortunately for those attackers, they were met with superior forces.

A few days after the riot, when tensions were still heightened, an organization known as the West Indian Standing Conference, with headquarters in Earls Court, forwarded information that Mr. Norman Washington Manley from Jamaica would be visiting the Notting Hill area to meet with West Indians. This brought a sense of excitement to the troubled community of black people.

On the day of his arrival, West Indians, Africans and some Indians gathered at Notting Hill from as far as Brixton, Kilburn, Fulham, Shepherd Bush, Paddington and of course Ladbrook Grove. They were eager to see and hear from the first Jamaican leader, one of two black leaders from the Caribbean, who came to hear and champion their cause. Like many Jamaicans I had knowledge of, but never met the great man before. My father often told stories of his legal achievements and his leadership of the People's National Party in Jamaica, but his coming to Great Britain to mediate in a racial upheaval was the action that fuelled my determination to rise and suppress the white notion of superiority.

After addressing the gathering, Mr. Manley invited us to walk with him through sections of Notting Hill in a show of solidarity. The procession took us from Notting Hill down through Kensington High Street and on towards Knightsbridge. On reaching Kensington High Street, the walk was stopped by police officers, who had arrived in their numbers and inquired who was heading the procession, to which the now-famous answer was given, and I quote: "I am Norman Washington Manley, Queen's Council."

Upon hearing those words, especially 'Queen's Council,' the police gradually stepped aside and allowed the peaceful march to continue. Many of us were not able to see and hear the events unfolding upfront, but the roar of joy reverberated throughout the entire community. This was the black man's finest hour and we were convinced that history was made on that day in September 1958.

But the unfolding of those momentous events, and my role and presence in them, had their genesis a few years earlier. Like many Jamaicans and Caribbean nationals of the so-called Windrush Generation, I had taken the opportunity to journey across the vast Atlantic to England, seeking opportunity. My desire was to study and become an engineer. But, unbeknownst to me then, the Master had quite a different plan for my life, as we shall discover.

Let us now go to the beginning of it all.

DEPARTURES & ARRIVALS

It was a bright and sunny day in the month of August 1955, when I arrived in London, along with over 100 other Jamaicans. The journey commenced in Kingston, Jamaica aboard a ship named the SS Castle Verde, an Italian registered vessel. "This magnificent-looking structure," I thought as I walked up its gangway, "will be taking me unto the great unknown, an adventure likened to the great explorers about whom we were taught at school."

Upon reaching the deck, of what was then to me, a huge floating house and looking out from the Kingston Harbour towards the sea, I suddenly became anxious from the thought of something happening to the vessel out on the ocean and me being unable to swim. What if I got sick on board? Who would look after me? And would I see my parents alive again?

Then moments later, the ship's horn bellowed out a thunderous sound alerting visitors and family members to go ashore as it prepared for departure. Gradually, the vessel began to move outwards to the ocean, but our eyes were not focused in that direction, but toward the Kingston Harbour, and the shores of Jamaica.

Everyone except the crew stood on the deck, waving and waving until the people ashore were out of sight. We then watched sadly as the shore itself disappeared from view. As the vessel proceeded further and further out on the ocean, many of my fellow passengers became seasick and for a long time could not even bear to see food, let alone eat it. This was a frightening experience for me as I watched them hanging over the rails of the deck, anxiously trying to bring something up from their stomach. Then suddenly it was dark, and there was nothing to see, but the lights on the ship. Looking outward, there was nothing; it was as if we were in a different space in a different time. Persons could be heard praying aloud for safe passage as we continued on our journey.

As morning broke, we rushed on deck to see if we could catch a glimpse of other passing vessels, or perhaps an island, but that was not to be. Only water everywhere. The circuitous journey took us past the majestic Rock of Gibraltar and then on to Barcelona, Spain; our first port of call. From there, we travelled to the port of Genoa in Italy where we disembarked. Our late arrival did not allow us to see much of the Italian port and its surroundings before night descended on us, and we were ushered onto a train, which was stationed adjacent to the port, waiting to take us on the next leg of the journey.

We travelled overnight through Italy and then unto the French port of Calais, where we alighted and boarded another vessel to take us across the English Channel, this time to the port of Dover, with its storied white cliffs, in England.

"At last," I thought as we disembarked. "Finally, I'm in England!" After 14 days of travelling over sea and land, we were anxious to reach our destinations and to meet with relatives and friends.

As we walked away from the ship, we were again guided to another train waiting in the station nearby. This would take us into London. On this leg of the journey, we were able to view and admire the beautiful English countryside, with its contoured slopes, unusual-looking animals grazing in the pastures, lush fields and gardens, and quaint-looking houses with chimneys atop. As we journeyed, I noticed that the pastures and the countryside were becoming smaller and smaller, while the houses were getting bigger and greater in number. Everyone's expectation was heightened as we neared London, figuring that we were finally reaching our "final "destination.

Suddenly the train whistled loudly, perhaps to signal that we were near the station, then gradually reduced its speed as we approached what, from the signs on the wall, was Victoria Station. We alighted from the train, clutching our various pieces of luggage, or "grips", as we called our suitcases at that time. We were all decked in our finest garments; the men wearing big-kneed pants, some with a jacket, and others with windbreakers and always a felt hat. The women wore the latest crinoline dresses, their hair well-groomed and iron-curled. We proceeded along the station's platform towards a group of uniformed persons who were awaiting our arrival. Upon our approach, it became clear that these persons were government officials. Some were immigration officers, customs officers and regular police officers who gave us directions to the various processing areas.

My close friend, Dee Clarke, who is not a relative, despite sharing a surname, stayed with me from when we started the journey at Norfolk Lane in Franklyn Town, Kingston. We remained together every step of the way until we entered the line before us, always clutching our treasured belongings. The immigration officer checked our passports, which, of course, were British passports and sent us on to customs, where each item we had was searched before we could enter the public domain. With suitcase in hand, I approached the custom officer who greeted me warmly, as he briefly went through my clothing. I had nothing to declare, so in no time I was standing aside waiting for my friend Dee to be processed. Then, in a fleeting moment, the most embarrassing experience a young man could ever encounter arriving in a strange place befell my friend as the custom officer inspected a piece of his luggage.

A few days before his departure, Dee had been sent an item from his aunt in St. Ann, to be taken to his uncle Clarence, who had left for England some months before and was living in Birmingham, which was Dee's final destination. This item was a large tin container, usually referred to as a "shut pan" securely wired down to protect its contents over the long journey. However, on reaching customs, this item of luggage had to be opened for inspection. The officer, armed with a wire cutter, proceeded to clip the wires from the container and slowly removing the cover suddenly gasped and jumped back while shouting, "Bloody hell, we have worms here too mate! You didn't have to bring any with you. What the hell have you got here?" By this time, the whole atmosphere was permeated with the stench of unimaginable dimensions that engulfed almost the entire train station.

Dee then realized that his considerate and loving aunt had sent some salted mackerel for her brother and nephew to enjoy on his arrival home in Birmingham. But after 14 days of travel, the only contents of the container were some of the largest worms you could behold! Instinctively, I removed myself from the scene, without even saying goodbye to my friend, not waiting to be associated with that embarrassing episode. I proceeded to one of the exits of the station to find my way to my place of residence in London.

As I approached the exit, my eyes were focused on the huge buildings in the foreground and how magnificent they looked. I thought, "Surely one of those would be my home. After all, this was London and London was my destination."

Standing outside the Victoria Station and looking around in great anxiety, I reached into my pocket for the only link to my new world, a piece of paper, with the address of the place at which I was to join my guardian who had arrived a few months before. His son had joined him only a few weeks before me. As I read the instructions once again, I came to the part where my mother had written, born out of her travelling experience, "If you are in doubt of finding your direction, ask a police to assist you."

Luckily for me, standing on the pavement a few yards from the station, were two policemen dressed in blue uniforms with their helmets on, as if waiting to help a desperate soul like me. I walked up to them and politely said "Good day." I then asked if they could assist me, to which one replied, "Certainly." Handing him the paper on which the address was written, I explained that I had just arrived in the country and was seeking information on how I could get to 12 Grettleton Road, London, W9.

He reached into his breast pocket and took out a small book and proceeded to turn each page, slowly, reading carefully to find the bus connections to the location. His fellow officer also assisted by pointing out the different routes to my destination from where we were. I was finally told to take a bus at the stop a few yards from the station, and to ask the conductor to let me off at Edgeware and Harrow Road stop. From there, I should go left onto Harrow Road to the bus stop, where I would take a number 662 bus to the Paddington Hospital stop. From there, I should seek further directions to get to Grettleton Road, which was very close to the hospital. I thanked them for their kind assistance and went to the bus stop.

As I walked away, I began to notice the various vehicles as they passed. Taxis were small and black and the buses were all red and had an upper deck. I found myself thinking, "I will not be going up there." The bus for the first leg of the journey arrived a few minutes later at the stop. On entering, I observed a long seat at the back where the conductor was standing. Naturally, I headed right there and sat next to him. I informed him of my intended stop, and asked him to let me know when I had arrived.

A few minutes later, he advised me that the next stop at Edgeware Road and Harrow Road intersection would be mine. Remembering the policeman's instructions, upon exiting the bus, I turned left on to Harrow Road where a few yards along, was the next bus stop. On its arrival, I noticed that this bus was different from the one that I was on before. It had a long wire stretching on top to a line with electrical sparks coming from it similar to the early tramcars in Jamaica. The only noticeable difference was, this bus had rubber wheels instead of iron ones. I learned that they were called trolleybuses.

I informed the conductor of my intended stop and sometime later, he signalled that the next stop was mine and echoed the words "Paddington Hospital."

I alighted from the bus and looked around for another policeman to ask further directions. But unfortunately, after almost half an hour, there was still no police in sight. Being too timid to approach the passersby who were all white, I thought, "My God, what do I do now?" It was at that moment that I saw an older, black woman walking towards me, as if in a hurry. But as she approached, a feeling of relief and joy overtook me, just to see another black face and the hope that she would be able to help me. Without any hesitation, I said "Good afternoon ma'am, could you assist me please?" She looked at me and said "You just come?" and I thought, 'Thank God, she's a Jamaican' and replied "Yes, ma'am." I handed her the piece of paper with the address and informed her that I was told that it would be in the area. Upon reading it she confirmed, saying "Yes, it is just down the road from here. I'm on my way to work, but come let me take you there."

I was overjoyed with the outpouring of kindness from this perfect stranger as she took my suitcase, and said "Follow me." We walked and chatted, mostly about Jamaica, until we reached the steps of the house that I was to be staying.

"This is it," she said and then walked up the steps in front of me and knocked on the door and waited. A short while later, the door gradually opened and to my great relief, I saw Rocky, the son of my guardian, standing there. Pointing to me, the woman asked him, "You know this young man?" When he responded in the affirmative, she said, "alright then, I goin' leave him with you."

I thanked her profusely for her kindness and wished her a good afternoon. To this point I had not even thought of asking her name. I was just happy to be home at last. The long journey was finally over! I was in England and I was settled.

As the day drew to a close, Rocky's father, having arrived from work, prepared the evening meal while he issued instructions on our activities for the following day. Chief among them was to visit the Labour Exchange to be registered for a job or Social Security benefits (aka the Dole).

Thereafter, we chatted for quite some time about Jamaica, and in particular, his wife and daughter who, very shortly, would join us in England. These people, the Pennycooks; Reckard and Rosa Pennycook and the children, Roxburgh (aka Rocky) and Verett, would now become my family. My parents and Maas Reckard and Miss Rosa, as they were affectionately called, were good friends, so when it became known that they were migrating to England, my mother asked them to care for me when I arrived.

The first night at my new home was somewhat uncomfortable. Having to share one room with two medium sized beds among the three of us was a new experience for me. In Jamaica, I had my own room and bed, a maid, and a 'yard boy' to do chores for me. "This will take a long time getting used to," I thought.

THE REAL WORLD

The next day my life in England really began. We were up at dawn. "I'm about to face the real world; the world of work and education, the world of becoming a man. What will I do, how will I survive away from the caring arms of my parents?"

As Maas Reckard prepared for work, he once again instructed us to go to the Labour Exchange to get registered. We were told which bus to take and the address of the Exchange. I had a few pounds in my pocket, so I wasn't worried about money, as yet.

We proceeded early to take the bus and to be the first in line at the Labour Exchange, which at the time, was located at Edgeware Road, not far from Marble Arch and the famous Hyde Park. On arrival, I was directed to join a line of job-seeking individuals, many of whom were immigrants from the other parts of the world such as Africa and Cyprus and of course, the West Indies. I was interviewed by a middle-aged, white lady who was very polite, but asked me many questions including my name, age, educational background and my reason for coming to England. I replied that my main intention was to become an engineer, but I wanted an opportunity to work as a motor mechanic to earn some money while attending school. When asked if I had any experience or qualifications as a motor mechanic, I informed her that I had six months' experience as an apprentice, but no qualifications. I had just completed 6 months at the John Crook garage on

Hanover Street in Kingston before leaving Jamaica and was considered a very good apprentice.

She looked at me, smiled broadly, and said, "In this country, you need to serve five years' apprenticeship to be employed as a mechanic." I immediately felt that my hopes of becoming an engineer via the mechanic route had just disappeared.

After looking through her files, I was advised that at the moment, the only suitable job available for someone like me, without any qualifications or experience, was a night job at the Walls Ice Cream Factory, located at a place called Acton. She further informed me that at age 18-21, the national wage was four pounds ten shillings per week. As far as I was concerned, this was a good job because it was the most money that I was going to earn in my short life.

With the offer having been accepted, she stamped a card and gave it to me to deliver to my employer when I arrived for work. Upon leaving the Labour Exchange, I sought directions to the factory to secure the job as soon as I could.

At the factory, the security directed me to the Personnel Department where I was once again asked a number of questions. The question, "When can you start?" was music to my ears. "As soon as it is possible," was my immediate response. I was then told to report for work the following night for the 10 pm to 6 am shift.

On the bus bound for home, it suddenly occurred that I would normally be asleep for the hours assigned for my shift. "How will I manage to keep awake?" I wondered. It was a frightening thought. Both Rocky and his father were happy for me getting a job so quickly.

The following day I woke up very early and looked forward to going to my first real job for which I would be getting paid. The hours went by slowly that day. I was so excited about this new job and spent all day wondering what my role would be. "Making ice cream..." I thought.

I reported to work at 9pm for the 10pm shift and was issued a coverall and a sanitary hat. I was told to go to the changing room and wait. From there, I would hear sirens signalling the end of the shift, then the foreman would direct me to my work area and show me what I was to do. I was placed with a work crew known as packers. We stood on either side of a conveyor belt, transporting various frozen ice cream products. We had to remove the assigned items from this continually moving device and pack them neatly into specially designed boxes for distribution. Within 15 minutes of handling the products both of my hands were numb and lifeless.

"What do I do now?" I wondered. "I just started my shift and I am unable to continue?" I frantically began rubbing my hands together, hoping to regain some feeling. Just then, a kind crew member pointed to a container with water under the conveyor belt and told me to stick my hands into it. Instantly, I stuck both hands way down in the container and realized seconds later that this was hot water, which was provided for such an occasion. I hastily removed my hands as life returned to them. This exercise was repeated several times throughout the shift that night. As morning broke and the shift ended I noticed that my hands had swollen to a frightening size, even though I felt no pain. I decided then and there that this was not the job for me.

On reaching home, I explained to Mr. Pennycook what had happened and inquired how I could terminate the job. "Just ask for your cards," he told me. The card which was given to me by the Labour Exchange, was now my employment card.

The following night, I went straight to the office and told the foreman that I wanted my cards, to which he remarked, "Ok, if that's what you want." The following morning at the end of the shift, I was handed an envelope containing my pay for two nights' work along with my cards. I had the shock of my life when I opened the envelope and saw the amount of money that was in it. This was much more than the four pounds ten shillings per week that was paid to persons under the age of 21. It was certainly much more than I had ever earned in my life and considering that I had only worked for two nights, I was tempted to change my mind about quitting the job.

But looking at my hands once again, I was convinced that I was doing the right thing.

The next few days were spent with Rocky exploring parts of London such as Hyde Park, Marble Arch and the West End, with its huge and beautifully decorated stores, each beckoning you to come in and spend some money. We travelled by bus and then by underground train. I decided moving deep underground with such speed and safety was a fantastic and fascinating experience.

Finally, after a few weeks, Mrs. Pennycook aka Ms. Rosa arrived and immediately took charge of the family affairs. Everyone was happy to be able to enjoy a good home-cooked meal again, even though the food was different from what we were accustomed to back in Jamaica. On the second day of her arrival, Ms. Rosa sent me to the shop which later became known to us as the green grocery shop, just down the corner from where we lived. I was told to buy two pounds of Irish potatoes for dinner.

As I approached the stall bearing various products, a stocky white man in a brown coat inquired of my needs. I looked across the aisle and saw two different colour potatoes, with a price tag on the stall indicating that one was for a penny per pound and the other for penny and a half, normally referred to as penny ha'penny. I told the grocer that I wanted two pounds of Irish potato, pointing to the one for a penny per pound.

To my great surprise, the goodly gentleman became enraged and began using the most vulgar expletives, while shouting aloud, "Irish, Irish potatoes? I have no 'effing' Irish potatoes, I have King Edwards, King Edwards! Irish, I have no damn potatoes!" Frightened by the sudden outburst, I ran from the shop, leaving behind the very thought of buying anything like potatoes.

On reaching home, aghast and frantically banging on the door to get in, Miss Rosa inquired what had happened as she opened the door. I recounted the incident as best as I could. She took the money from me and proceeded to the shop to purchase the potatoes. Over time, we became aware of the fragile and troubled relationship which existed between some of our Irish friends and the English people.

Ms. Rosa and I secured jobs at a small Polish sausage packing company very near to our home on Malvern Road, W9, where my job function was to pack sausages for delivery. The pay of course, was four pounds ten shillings per week, out of which I made my contribution towards groceries and rent. By this time, Verett had joined us, so the family had moved to a much larger and more convenient accommodation at Elcome Street off the Westburne Park Road, Paddington W9. We now occupied two large, furnished rooms, and a kitchen. It was at this new address that I began to experience the true meaning of adulthood.

Although the space at this new address was bigger, the household had grown. In addition to the four Pennycooks, Mr. Sidney Blake, affectionately called Syd, from Malvern, St. Elizabeth who was an old friend of the Pennycook's, had asked to be accommodated there on his arrival. I was now faced with the new experience of sleeping three in a bed. Rocky, Syd and I occupied one room while the Pennycook family occupied the other.

It was about the month of October that the weather began gradually changing from chilly to cold. Fortunately, all of us were working except Verett, so we were able to contribute adequately to rent, food and heating.

The rooms had two huge fireplaces, which was the conventional way of heating at that time. We were able to purchase a bag of coal, which we stored in the basement of the building, from the coal man who would pass by on his donkey cart at least once a week. The cost was five shillings per bag. We also purchased what was known then as a paraffin heater which we used in the kitchen. Every evening, the first person who arrived from work would make a fire to warm up the rooms. At nightfall, the family would gather in the room that was occupied by the three males to talk about the day at work and quite often would move on to Jamaica and who and what we missed. Since we had no radio, television or telephone, our main past-time was to sit before the fireplace and converse with each other.

The first night of the cold spell, I insisted that I would sleep at the front of the bed facing the fireplace and Rocky and Syd agreed. I woke up the next morning with cold blisters on my body and had to seek medical attention at the Paddington Hospital. I was told that as the fire waned during the early morning the temperature dropped to chilly or cold and this resulted in blisters on the body, especially if you were very near to the fire all night. Armed with this knowledge, I suggested that the bed be shifted, and asked to be given the corner slot. My roommates agreed.

I was still working at the sausage factory as the month of October drew to an end. One day, I went to work for my usual shift, which began at 8 am and ended at 4:30 pm. As usual, having spent the entire day in the basement of the building, I emerged all dressed up, ready to go home only to find that it was dark outside. Just the previous day I had, at that time, found a very bright evening. I ran back downstairs and shouted that something was wrong and some bad event had befallen London. Everyone began to laugh loudly at my ignorance and laughingly remarked that the clock had been adjusted for the winter season.

As I walked home that evening, I began to feel very sad. Being laughed at was quite unusual for me and I made a vow to inform myself of the customs and the practices of the country of my new residence. I also promised that I would become knowledgeable about as many things relating to London that I could, so as not to find myself in such a position again.

By November, the weather became much colder than I had ever experienced even though I resided in Potsdam, (where Munro College is situated) in St. Elizabeth, Jamaica, which is considered one of the coldest places in the island especially toward the end of December through to February each year. Rocky and I, realizing that we were inadequately prepared for this period with the windbreakers that we had, took the opportunity when a door-to-door salesman knocked on our door to interest us in purchasing various items from The Littlewoods catalogue. That was the popular purchasing method for garments and household items and such delights. It offered a hire purchase weekly plan commonly known as the "Never, never plan." It was called 'never never' because even when the article is finished or destroyed, you would still be paying for it.

Upon going through the catalogue, we saw articles that we were in need of; chief among them was the overcoat that would keep us warm for the winter. The one that we chose was a dual-purpose coat which could be worn as a raincoat during the summer, simply by unzipping the flannel lining from it. We decided right then and there to enter this plan because we had insufficient money to purchase the items. This meant that we were able to choose other items to prepare for the winter. I also got a pair of gloves, a scarf and two pairs of thick socks. The overcoat cost ten guineas (now approximately ten pounds ten shillings), as it was called then and the salesman wondered why we chose such an expensive one. But we were determined that we wanted the best so that we could keep as warm as possible.

The clothing brought from Jamaica was not appropriate for that time of the year, or fashion-wise, as suits were worn by almost everyone. I had yet to acquire one because it could not be afforded on my salary. We expressed our concern to Mr. Pennycook, who advised us to go to Burton's Tailoring at the corner of Harrow Road and Twickenham Road, where we would be able to get made-to-measure suits on a weekly payment plan and he would stand as guarantor for us.

The next day, we proceeded to the tailoring store, got measured and expressed the urgency of our need as we wanted to be prepared for the Christmas season. By the first week of December, I was decked out in my new suit and overcoat and felt hat of course, and the thought that I was now moving up in the world.

Christmas was fast approaching and excitement was in the air. It was snowing and I intended to make the best of my first Christmas away from Jamaica. But money had become a concern, as I had to pay the weekly hire purchase installments in addition to rent and food and heat. Four pounds ten shillings a week could not cut it.

But, as if the good Lord was looking down on me, someone told me about an upcoming vacancy for a porter at the Paddington Hospital. Two days later, I went to the hospital and met with Mr. Reeder, the personnel manager, who looked at my attire, which was my whole new outfit and asked a few questions including 'Where I was from?' And listening quite attentively to my almost perfect English, he decided that I would be given the job.

To this point, I had no idea of the role of a porter, which was the position being filled, but when I was told that the pay was eight pounds ten shillings per week with lunch, I was so overjoyed, my only question was, "When do I start?" He told me to report for work the next Monday morning at 7. I then went back to my work place and asked for my cards, which I received the following Friday evening. By now, everyone at home had become excited about my new pay scale which would make me one of, if not the highest-paid member of the household. I set about preparing for my new and exciting job as a porter, while wondering what it entailed.

That Sunday night, I set the clock to alarm at 6 am, which would give me enough time to walk to the hospital which was not far away. On arrival, I was introduced to an elderly Scotsman by the name of Jack Mulholland, who I was to replace in a short time. I was escorted to the kitchen to meet some members of the staff, and in particular, the person who was in charge and who would be my immediate boss. I was introduced to a fat, English woman with a bandage on her right leg. I was informed by her that my duties were to prepare potatoes, Irish potatoes if you will, better known as spuds to meet the entire hospital's needs on a daily basis. I was also informed that the various requirements would be posted on the menu sheet the day before. All this would be shown to me by Jack.

My first assignment, after changing into my overalls, was to carry a number of hundred-pound bags of potatoes on my back from the cellar to the preparation room for processing. Each sack was emptied into a large drum with rough edges inside and an electrically revolving base, which when filled with water would remove the skin of the potatoes.

After approximately three minutes, one would then empty the contents into a large container for final peeling and cleaning using a very sharp knife in the process. The cleaned potatoes would then be prepared according to the menu and placed into various large containers with water. Some were sliced for crisps, some diced for chips (known as French fries in other places) and whole potatoes for table or mash.

The weather was now becoming a worrisome situation. It was much colder and I began to wear as much clothing as my body could support, whether going to work even at home. I would be awakened early in the mornings only to find the coal fire had died and the temperature in the room had dropped significantly. I'd hasten to put on a vest, then a shirt, pants, a pair of socks, a jacket, a scarf, my shoes, an overcoat and gloves and a hat or cap and then off to work I would go. At work, I would get a cup of hot tea and naturally, a warmer temperature.

As the days went by and the weather got worse, I found myself in what could be described as survival state. The pipes at home were frozen, which meant an inadequate or non-existent water supply. Sometimes, there was no coal to burn, only a paraffin heater to keep the room warm. I would reach home late in the evenings, because the warmer atmosphere at work was much more accommodating. When I got home, I would remove only my hat and shoes and then go straight to bed. I'd get up early the next morning with the awful smell of paraffin all over my clothes from the fumes generated when we burned the product. I had to endure this embarrassing situation for some time. With snow on the ground and the pipes frozen, we had to adopt new methods of hygiene such as filling a saucepan with snow, melting it on the stove then leaving it to cool. This provided some water to wipe down, but not to drink, maybe particularly because melted snow tasted very bitter.

Elcome Street was situated in one of the older areas of Paddington, and the houses all had lead piping, which froze easily in severely cold weather. This state of affairs began to frustrate me, as I was accustomed to proper hygiene, which included having regular baths. Realizing that I had not enjoyed a bath since the weather had changed, made me unhappy and uncomfortable.

I therefore welcomed the information that there was a public bathing and swimming facility not far from where I was living. The facility, my colleague explained, was equipped to provide service all year round for bathing and swimming in all kinds of weather. There I could get a proper bath.

With this information and excited at the prospect of enjoying a bath and feeling clean again, I eagerly made my way to Ha'penny, Steps, off the Harrow Road, West 9. "Thank God," I said, when I got there.

On entering the building, I was directed to the cashier's cage where I paid sixpence for the bath and then handed a rag and a small cake of soap. As I proceeded to the bathing area down the passageway I was surprised to find that though the temperature inside was adequately warm, my hands and feet were very cold, almost freezing.

As I walked down the passageway, I noticed a number of men lining up to sit on the benches that were placed together to form one continuous stretch of seats for the intended bathers. I stood beside the person who had entered before me, and gradually moved when a voice at the far end of the benches shouted out, "Next!" Naturally, having waited my turn, when the seat became vacant, I placed myself to await the call for my opportunity to go to the bathing room.

After some time moving gradually down on the benches, I found myself at the end, meaning my wait was almost finally over. I was eager to take a good bath. Thank God, I would go next.

I was advised that if you gave the attendant a small tip, even a tuppence, you would be sure of getting extra water in the tub which enabled you to relax and enjoy as much of the warmth as possible. I did not have a tuppence, so on entering the cubicle I handed him a sixpence. To my great joy, he handed me a large towel and almost filled the tub to the brim with water, for which I was so happy.

To him, the sixpence was a large sum of money, and therefore he was more than happy to make me feel comfortable and I was pleased to get so much water. When I went in, I quickly dipped my hands in to test the temperature. As my hands were so cold at the time the water seemed just about above room temperature. I proceeded to step into the tub, which again, felt normal because my feet were also very cold, almost frozen. I lathered copiously then decided to recline for a few minutes in the tub just to soak my body properly.

Unfortunately, as the temperature of my upper body was normal, and not frozen like my extremities, upon contact, I realized too late that the water was piping hot. As it seared my testicles and my buttocks I knew that was not the experience that I had anticipated. My screams, which must have been heard throughout the entire building and perhaps the surrounding area, speedily brought the attendant and other persons who were waiting to take their turn to bathe, to the cubicle anxiously inquiring what was the matter. Having described my ordeal to the attendant, he added some cold water to allow me to enjoy a comfortable and cleansing bath, but I already felt sore between my legs and my buttocks. My journey home was very uncomfortable, and I had to walk with my legs as far apart as possible to avoid the burning sensation that I felt when I tried to walk normally.

Upon being told of my ordeal, Rocky rushed to the shop to purchase some butter to apply to my affected parts. But butter was on ration, so he had to settle for a tin of Vaseline. For a number of days, I hopped around at all times and tried to get myself back to normal. I also prayed especially that my manhood was not impaired.

As Christmas drew nearer, everyone in the family began preparing for their first one away from Jamaica. With all the excitement in the air, we wanted to make the best of it, despite the difficulties we had experienced so far. It was then that I bought and tasted my first bottle of whiskey. At fifteen shillings per bottle; *Teachers* whiskey was surprisingly good at keeping the body warm.

We decided to stock up on produce for the Christmas season, but unfortunately we could not purchase any perishable goods as we had no refrigerator. Rabbit, lamb, chicken and horse meat were available. One could not tell that it was horse meat because it was normally so beautifully cut, it caught the eye first. Beef was more expensive and scarce because it was sent to feed soldiers on the front line, so we had to make do with what we had, certainly, however, not horse meat. Many persons that I knew were fooled into believing that they had been buying beef. Bottles of milk, eggs and bread, which we could get unsliced and unwrapped, were delivered by the milkman who would leave items on the step, by the door, if no one was there, which was usually the case.

We knew when the delivery man was coming because we could hear him several blocks away down the road with his donkey cart. We made sure to purchase at least two bags of coal and potatoes, which was the only staple ground provision. There was no yam, no sweet potatoes, nothing else that we were accustomed to in Jamaica.

On Christmas Eve, which fell on a Saturday that year, Rocky and I decided to have some fun, and in particular to go dancing. We were advised that the best place to go for that occasion was the Hammersmith Palais, which was only two train stations away from where we lived. The rest of the family decided to go to a nearby pub on the Westburne Park Road. As the evening approached, we rushed over to the public bath to get all cleaned up and refreshed, making sure this time that the water temperature was right for me. After an enjoyable bath, we proceeded home to get dressed in our latest suit, and looked forward to meeting some nice girls and dancing the rest of the night away.

DISAPPOINTMENT

W e arrived at the Hammersmith Palais to the sound of music. Having paid the entrance fee and checked in our overcoats, we proceeded straight to the bar near the ballroom, which was very well attended. We noticed that most attendees were couples, but there were some unattached females. At the bar, we noticed that all eyes were on us and wondered, why all this attention? Suddenly, we realized that we were the only non-white persons in the place. At the bar we ordered two tins of Tennant Beer, which was the popular drink back then. We drank quickly and tried to ease the discomfort we were now experiencing. After another round of beer, we walked towards the dancing area, noting that the unattached ladies turned their backs on us as we moved along the outskirts of the dancing floor.

We also noticed that the music was not what we were accustomed to and certainly not for dancing. People were dancing fox-trot, and waltz, played by the Joe Loss Orchestra, so even if we had the remotest chance of getting a dance partner, we would not have known what to do, or which move to make. Eventually, after hanging around for three quarters of an hour, we decided to return home. Such was our experience of the Hammersmith Palais on a Saturday night in 1955.

The return trip required only one train from the Hammersmith Station to Westburne Park Station, which was close to our home. As we walked up

Westburne Park Road towards Harrow Road and approached the bridge at the intersection of Elcome Street, we noticed someone laying on the sidewalk and heard a female shouting for "help." We rushed towards them only to discover that the person laying on the ground was our roommate, Syd, and he was surrounded by a pool of blood. The person shouting for help was Rocky's sister, Verett. Shocked, and believing he was dead, we asked what had happened. We were told that four young men dressed in black had approached them while they were returning from the pub, shouting, "You black bastards, go home to your effing jungle, we don't want your effing kind here!"

They immediately started hitting Syd on his forehead with what appeared to be a bicycle chain, and another with a knuckle duster. After hearing the story, Rocky and I decided to take him to the house, which was just a few steps away, when suddenly, Syd started groaning, moving his hands naturally towards his head. We told him to take it easy, whilst gently helping him to his feet. Supporting him on either side we walked slowly to the house. As we approached, we saw Rocky's father and mother on the steps. Rocky's dad was prostrate on the ground, and his mom was crying aloud. I felt numb with horror as I watched and listened to the unfolding events. Mr. Pennycook was soaked in blood oozing from his forehead, having earlier met the same set of young men on the way home.

Having gone to have a drink to celebrate their first Christmas Eve in England at the nearby pub on Westbourne Park Road on their return home they were not walking together as a group, as Mr. & Mrs. Pennycook were ahead. This perhaps made both groups easier targets for the vicious young men.

The noise got the attention of our two closest neighbours, who were white. They assisted us by calling the ambulance from their house phone. When told of the horrifying event, they explained to us that this was the action of the Teddy Boys, a group of young men identifiable by the black outfit they wore, akin to the black shirts of the Mosleyites. The Mosleyites were a collection of fascist and racist organizations inhabiting parts of England and followers of 1940s British fascist Sir Oswald Mosley. The Teddy Boys had a reputation for being vicious. They were also known to launch their attacks on single black males in particular or small groups of persons, especially at nights. They always travelled in packs of no less than four. The ambulance arrived shortly after and took both men to St. Charles Hospital in Ladbrook Grove, where they were admitted in serious condition. All my hopes of a nice first Christmas in England were totally destroyed. I turned my focus on helping my guardians get back in good health. We visited the hospital regularly and offered our prayers, and comfort.

As the days passed, the horrifying events became etched in my mind accompanied by an anger that I had never felt in my lifetime. I wanted to hurt someone, or even kill in reprisal for this brutal act against innocent and unsuspecting people. My great anger was also shared by Rocky and we decided that we should arm ourselves. We needed to be proactive and ready to protect ourselves from the now obvious expectation of racially motivated attacks from the Teddy boys.

On the Wednesday following the Christmas holiday we proceeded to execute our plan. A store on Praed Street opposite the Paddington railway station which sold switchblade knives was our destination. No questions were asked as we sought to obtain two knives with the largest and the longest blades. To keep them sharp and shiny we also bought a sharpening stone. We spent many hours the following weeks honing them to perfection. They were so sharp that you could cut the breeze. They became our abiding companion and were carried on our person everywhere we went day and night.

Mr. Pennycook and Sydney had spent four weeks in the hospital, but thankfully, their wounds had healed and they were now back at work. Family life had returned to normal, but the winter was still severe and our routine of keeping warm and bathing at an offsite facility continued.

With everything that had transpired, Elcome Street seemed to be the worst place to live, so we started to seek new accommodation. The bitter cold passed slowly as the month of February progressed. On the streets and in stores, we began meeting more and more black people. Naturally, there was mutual happiness to meet fellow Jamaicans and become acquainted irrespective of where they were from. We shared our experiences about life in our new country and advised whether there were any available jobs or vacant rooms, which were always in demand by most of our friends at the time.

My job at the hospital was still going well and the decent wages allowed me to acquire more suits, shoes, shirts and ties. My attire caught the attention of not only older ladies, but older men. The ladies admired me for being smartly-dressed and the men, for the way my tie fitted. Most of them had never worn a tie in their life and therefore could not tie one. Soon that admiration led to a side job in which I found myself on weekends tying ties for several people. I charged sixpence per tie. Luckily for me, my father wore a jacket and tie almost everywhere in Jamaica and had taught me the art of tying ties.

As there was no barber around to service the black community, I also found myself cutting my friends and colleagues' hair on occasion. This would sometimes result in the person having to wear a hat until the hair grew back a bit. But it was all done in good spirit and a desire to help each other out.

Notwithstanding these new developments, Rocky and I still had not fully gotten over our disappointing holiday experience. We also agreed that family time needed other elements besides reminiscing to add some enjoyment, so off we went to rectify that problem. At the corner of Twickenham Road and Shirland Road was a small music shop, which was owned by an Irishman, who later became a close friend. There, in exchange for a whopping seventeen pounds, we got a record player. Of course, a record player is no good without records and so a 78 Calypso record titled "Night Food," which cost twelve shillings and sixpence, was added to our purchase.

It was a Saturday afternoon and everyone was at home and I intended to surprise them with some good Jamaican music. I hurried home very excited and plugged in the extension cord, then placed the record on the turntable and to their surprise and joy the sound of Jamaica was in the air. We took the arm of the record player off the turntable to allow the record to repeat automatically. Everyone danced to the one tune the entire evening. At one point we heard a knocking on the door and thought the neighbours were coming to complain, but it turned out to be a Jamaican who was passing from work and heard the music. He wanted to know how he could obtain one of those records. He was invited to stop for a while, but declined the offer, stating that he would rather like to go home and freshen up and then bring his wife back with him later, if that was okay. The Pennycook family was a fun-loving group of people, always happy to make new friends, so naturally they said yes.

Sometime later the couple came, bringing with them a bottle of *Teacher's* whiskey and that was the beginning of a party that continued all through that night until early the next morning. Little did we realize that one event would characterize our lifestyle for many years.

The man and his wife became lifelong friends and everyone felt that this was the beginning of many months and years of happiness in England.

The events of the night led me to conclude that other Jamaicans in the area might not be aware of this record and its availability, so I decided that I would contact the owner of the music shop to arrange to sell this and all other future Calypso records on a commission basis.

The following week we came to a gentlemen's agreement to sell these and other records and closed the deal with the shaking of hands. I also left with six copies of "Night Food." As I embarked on my sales journey I was pleasantly surprised to learn that many Jamaicans and other West Indians had purchased radiograms and record players of varying sizes, mostly on a hire purchase plan. This was good news for me as it made it very easy for me to dispose of my records, which I sold for seventeen shillings and sixpence. I earned five shillings from each record sold and I thought I was in good business. With sales happening quickly, I began to expand my base and variety, which by now had included "Water the Garden"; among others. Things were going very well, or so I thought, when suddenly and unfortunately for me, my friend had to close the business. I later became aware that many other places started selling Calypso and other West Indian records. People were also making direct purchases from these stores and therefore even for me, business was not as good as it was before, so I also abandoned selling records.

Around the same time, I had a pleasant surprise. I was on my way out to work one morning when on the stairs of my apartment I ran into another of my very best friends from Jamaica. Edward Levy had just arrived the previous day and coincidentally was staying upstairs the very same building that we were trying to vacate. How happy I was to see my old schoolmate and friend in England.

Fortunately for Eddie, there was a vacancy for a porter at the hospital where I worked and on my recommendation he got the job. His role was to prepare vegetables while I prepared potatoes for the meals served at the hospital. Gainfully employed, he joined us as we intensified our search for new accommodation, but the harsh reality of racial discrimination began to emerge. Notices for vacant rooms would normally be placed in the front windows of those houses. They now read, "No Irish, no blacks, no dogs." Some would state, "No niggers, and no Coloureds." This experience was a shocking one for me, especially since I was born in the parish St Elizabeth to a father of Scottish descent. My paternal grandmother had immigrated to Jamaica from Scotland and married into a family in Santa Cruz. I grew up in South Saint Elizabeth with friends and acquaintances in Queensbury, Southfield, Ballards Valley and Warminster to name a few of the areas with families of Scottish descent. Likewise, Mr. Pennycook who was the descendant of Charles Pennycook, a white man who had migrated to Jamaica along with his brothers from Scotland. They had settled in Warminster. This discrimination was therefore almost demoralizing to us as a family, but we were determined to improve our living conditions so the search continued. It was not until the month of May 1956, that we were able to find a new place to live. Our new address was 98 Sutherland Avenue, near the Maidavale underground station and within walking distance from the Lord's cricket ground. I felt like I was in heaven. Not only because I was a great cricket fan, but also, this was one of the most upscale areas in the Paddington and surrounding areas.

The house was bought part vacant by Mr. Roy Francis, a good friend of the family, whose wife was also from Saint Elizabeth. Naturally, we were very happy to be offered residence at that location. Rocky, Eddie and I shared the largest room on the first floor and Mr. and Mrs. Pennycook and

Verett had their dwelling on the 2nd floor. Our good friend Sydney went to live in Slough, not far from Heathrow Airport. Everyone was comfortable at last. This is where I began to enjoy life as a young adult, earning a good pay that enabled me to purchase what I needed and making new friends, especially ladies who were always much older than me. I was going out to parties on the weekends and always going to the movies. There were hardly any black or coloured girls, as they were called then, around at that time and especially those of our age group as teenagers. The few who would be available went out with American servicemen, GIs, as they were called, who had money, unlike young West Indians whose earnings would not be close to that of an American soldier.

Older black men would find friendship with unattached prostitutes who they would meet at the pubs, or females at their workplaces. Younger girls, even young prostitutes, were totally out of the reach of black boys like us.

My newfound enjoyment did not last very long. An Englishman was recruited as my assistant, and within a few weeks of employment began preparing the potatoes in a manner which was unacceptable to management. His preparation did not follow the menu requirements and resulted in numerous complaints that I was not aware of, until very late. I was blamed for what had occurred and was eventually dismissed from the job.

I realized then, that the issue was that the Englishman was not prepared to work under the supervision of a black man and accordingly the management, in the person of the HR manager, took the view that it would be better for me as a black person to go instead of dismissing his white counterpart.

It was a sad experience to be fired from a job knowing it was racially motivated as I had performed consistently without any complaints before. Still in shock, I collected my cards and my pay that Friday evening without any question. After that, I met Rocky at the cinema, which we called "Bug House," located just a few yards from the hospital to enjoy one of our favourite cowboy movies.

A NEW EXPERIENCE

The following Monday I took the underground train from Madavale Station to Regent Park. This was the first leg of my journey to West End London to find employment. Having alighted the train I walked along Great Portland Street towards Oxford Street, which was quite a new venture for me, as I had never visited that area before. Just after passing the dental hospital, I arrived at a building with a sign which read "Solomon Levy" and in brackets "SL Handbags." Then a notice in the window caught my eye. "Packer/Warehouse Man Wanted." I paused long enough to wonder what this job entailed then decided, "It cannot be worse than peeling potatoes!"

I entered, and an elderly gentleman met me at the door and inquired how he could help. "The notice in the window brought me in," I informed him, "and I wondered if I could fulfill the requirement". He smiled at me and said, "A young lad like you, we could give you a try." He then invited me upstairs to the office for an interview and at the end offered me the job. I agreed to start the very next day. The Tuesday morning at work, Sam, the elderly gentleman I'd met the day before, introduced me to the rest of the staff and then to some of the owners of the business. He informed me that the business was owned by a close Jewish family and everyone working there was treated as family. In 1956, there were hardly any black persons working in the West End area of London. Most immigrants, who were usually older, secured jobs in factories, on the railway, or on buses as conductors so I was pleasantly surprised at the welcome I received from an all-white working group. Everyone on staff was called by their first name and the owners as Mr. and Miss. The company was owned by the Levys: Alfred Levy or Sir Alfred as we called him, who was the eldest; Monty, Leonard and Doris Levy. They were siblings. To my joy, the job turned out to be less hectic than the previous one. My role was to carry handbags from the storeroom in the basement to the first floor where they would be packed in large carton boxes by a packing expert, named Joe. I then sealed and taped the boxes. We wore brown coveralls which were maintained by the company.

Just three weeks later, Sam decided to promote me to postal clerk, a position in which I would oversee small packages of handbags going through the post office. I was not aware that during the three weeks the family was observing my 'command of the English language' and felt that I could be of greater use to the company and doing more than just sealing boxes. Before long, I was delivering sample handbags and small packages to handbag buyers in the various department stores in London West End and beyond. The client base included established top retailers such as Selfridges, Swan and Edgars, Dolcies, Saxoone, DH Evans, Harrods in Knightsbridge, Marks & Spencer, John Lewis among others. This job did not pay as much as the previous one, but who cared? I was living a good life. A taxi took me to my destination for every delivery. Always well-suited, I interacted with very important and beautiful ladies who were in charge of the particular departments. I was enjoying the job so much, I even forgot about my intentions to study to become an engineer.

The handbags were manufactured in the SL factory in the East End of London and then delivered to Great Portland Street headquarters, which was the distribution centre. My rapid ascendancy created a vacancy for a warehouse packer. The position was filled by another young black man by the name of Edwin Dejinu, a Ghanaian who came to England to study shipping. We immediately became friends and spent a lot of time together.

At the various department stores my popularity grew with every visit. The buyers and other members of staff engaged me in conversation to ascertain where I came from, where I learnt to speak English, which college I attended, and how I was able to dress so immaculately all the time. I found it most disturbing that on saying I was from Jamaica, the most frequent follow-up question was, "Where in Africa is that?" I would usually become upset at that point, but eventually concluded that the standard of education, especially among the working class, was not as high as we in Jamaica perceived it to be. Eventually, I deduced that when those in senior positions in the establishments entertained a conversation, it was done in an attempt to demonstrate a white superior knowledge over a little black man coming from a third world depressed country who expressed himself above the ordinary. As such, I began to resent their approach in engaging me in these conversations knowing full well their intentions. I very quickly realized the subtle manner in which the racial undercurrent was being exercised by those in positions of authority and took a vow never to be subordinated because of my colour.

THE VOW

In that vow I adopted the phrase, "If you can't beat them, join them," to which I added ***learn from them and then beat them at their own game***. To achieve this objective, I started reading about the British culture and at the same time meeting with other young black men from Africa, and the West Indies to include Guyanese, Barbadians, Trinidadians, and Grenadians, which were very few then. We shared experiences as we went about our daily lives and formed close friendships, most of which lasted many years.

We regarded ourselves as revolutionaries, with our vision and mission geared towards the upliftment of young, black men in England. We also formed a musical band and on weekends performed at various halls catering to the coloured population. The band leader, who also played the clarinet, was from Jamaica; the saxophonist was from Guyana; guitarist from Barbados; drummer from Jamaica, specifically Top Hill in St. Elizabeth; and yours truly the vocalist. Our ultimate performance was at the Brixton Town Hall prior to the advent of the sound system era, which was beginning to dominate the musical entertainment space. My exposure to the musical world once again ignited my passion for dancing, which became one of the hallmarks of my life, even to this day.

The rock 'n' roll era had started and house parties proved to be highly convenient as a means of entertainment after a hard week's work for us coloureds. It did not take much to have a party in those days. If we went along the streets and heard music being played at a house, especially on a Saturday evening, we'd show up with a bottle and be welcomed.

My dancing prowess was admired at every party I attended. It brought so much pleasure that my friends encouraged me to do it professionally. My Ghanaian friend, Edwin, even invited me to perform at the Ghana Independence Celebration at the Seymour Hall near Marble Arch in March 1957, but I graciously declined.

London had suddenly become my oyster. Life was exciting. I was inquisitive and blessed with a determination to succeed in whatever I did. I wanted to be the best; the best dancer, the best dresser, the best speaker of English and the best worker. Serendipitously, I was informed of the existence of the first West Indian barber shop in Ladbrook Grove area, catering to all black men from various parts of London. Naturally, I did not hesitate to visit and get a proper haircut from professionals. This helped to further sharpen my image and move me in the right direction of looking my best. The business, operated by Aston and Joe, two Jamaicans, became the popular meeting place for discussions on issues of the Caribbean and the world. These visits for me became a very important part of my learning process. This interaction was a great segue to my job, which afforded me the opportunity to know various places and interact with many persons in the greater London area, which the vast majority of West Indians were not able to experience at that time.

To round out my informal education, after work, an hour or two at the library was commonplace for me, and then some fun with Rocky and Eddie.

1957 was a good and exciting year for us. Our group of close friends increased and were later even dubbed the "Necktie Gang" because of our immaculate way of dressing and our resolve to protect each other. We always went out together, knowing the perilous situation that existed in London if you ventured out on your own.

MY NEW ABODE

The Pennycooks finally saved enough money to deposit on a house in Harlesden, a large district in the then known borough of Willesden in Northwest London. Thankfully, it was vacant and we were able to move from Sutherland Avenue almost immediately after the riot. Unfortunately, the commute between West End and my new home was rather expensive and forced me to adjust my lifestyle in order to meet my basic needs. I chose to concentrate on improving my knowledge of British culture and studying as much as I could by visiting the local library at Craven Park in Harlesden after leaving work in the evenings.

But the adjustment to my lifestyle did not last very long after discovering that there was a nightclub, called the 31 Club, just two streets away from my new home. It was owned by a fellow St. Elizabeth son by the name Bob Elliot, and it was too difficult for me to resist. I started going to the club regularly, on every occasion I got, except Sundays. This turn of events caused me to neglect my usual prompt attendance to work and my responsibilities of writing home to my parents on a regular basis and even sending money for them. The end result was that I lost my job in the West End, and then, as if to further punish me, I learned in late December 1958 that my mother had died. She had adopted me, loved me and cared for me since I was three months old. I was devastated! I felt as if my world had come to an end and I wanted to die too, but didn't have the courage to bring it to pass. I cried non-stop for almost one month, and periodically thereafter when I reflected on my negligence towards them as well as my little sister Sheila. I recalled my mother saying to me on the day that I took the bus for Kingston to depart to England, "Spend three years my darling son, I love you."

1958 was not really a good year for me, but thank God in early January 1959 I was lucky enough to secure a job as a warehouse man at MoByke Accessories in Kilburn. The company was owned by a German named Mr. Binn. It was a small company with a staff complement of about six persons and once again, I was the only black person to be employed. My duties were to fill the orders from the various stores and to offload the parts brought by the delivery truck, and pack them in the store room. The storeroom, however, was not very large and so was very congested. The inventory was not placed in specific areas so finding items sometimes required searching the entire store, which made the job very difficult and time consuming. So when business was slow, I would go upstairs to the storeroom and rearrange the items by sequence and part number, thereby creating more space and making items easier to find when orders were to be filled.

The new system met mixed results in that it caused some problems for the older employees, but was a great delight to Mr. Binn. Within three months of my employment, he promoted me to supervisor, much to the resentment of the person I replaced. A couple of the staff were not onboard, and they wanted nothing to do with me and refused to take instructions at first, but eventually came to accept the boss' decision. I sometimes wondered then if I were given the position with the intention to see me fail. But from my experience with the job in the hospital, I endeavoured to make a success of whatever role I was called upon to do. After all, I believed that I was a people person.

Eventually, my relationship with all the staff became very good, but more so, my relationship with the boss. This was an excellent and very happy relationship. He would call me about everything concerning the employees and the stock. I was really enjoying this job. My pay scale had increased significantly, my period of mourning was coming to an end and my lifestyle was back on track. I even started to learn tap dancing on the weekends.

In early 1958, we went to a dance at the community hall in Kilburn, which was promoted by King B, one of the early sound systems in London. The entry fee was two shillings and sixpence, or half a crown as it was usually referred to then. Upon arrival, we went straight to the bar to have a few rounds of drinks before going to the dance floor. Our practice was to observe the females present from a distance; how they looked and how they danced. Suddenly, Rocky nudged me to look across from the bar where two beautiful young, black girls were standing. One, a shade darker than the other, but both were very pretty. I immediately walked over and wished them a good night and politely asked the one I considered prettier for a dance. She hesitated for a while, and then extended her hands in acceptance and we entered the dance floor.

At this point, all my friends stood watching in anticipation of the performance which would impress the young ladies. My favourite genre of rock 'n' roll and blues were playing and I was confident of my ability on the floor. After dancing to two tunes, and seeing a circle of people around us, the young lady was embarrassed and evidently wanted to leave the dance floor. But before I could thank her for the dance, I felt a hard slap on the left side of my face, which echoed across the hall. In great surprise, I rubbed the spot while walking her back to her friend, who turned out to be her cousin. Strangely, we became close after that slap. We danced many more times and then I walked her home at 2 am in the morning. Eventually, because of that occasion, she became my first love in London. We were inseparable for quite a while. Her brother and uncle also eventually became a part of the Necktie Gang and that relationship lasted for many years.

The group had expanded to include guys like Darrel Blackwood, popularly known as Doctor who hailed from Clarendon; Dudley McBean, from the Montego Bay area; John and Neville Brown from Kingston and Rocky, Edward "Eddie" Levy and I were all from St. Elizabeth The latest addition to the group, Alfonso, had migrated from Jamaica just that year. More popularly known as Needles, Alfonso was one of the greatest dancers that I ever met and we had the great honour of complimenting each other on the dance floor with the ladies on the occasions when we all went out to parties.

We became known as the "Necktie Gang" because of our mode of dressing, always in full suit and tie, which in my case was every day. Once again, I was enjoying life. My popularity had grown because of my dancing prowess, and local and international affairs had become one of my great passions, especially since the Notting Hill riot. As we ushered in the year 1960, I visited the library in Craven Park one evening after leaving work, as always. On this occasion, I decided to read a recently published newspaper, featuring an article on someone who was described as 'London's most flamboyant dresser.' His name was Nubar Gulbenkain, a business magnate and socialite who wore an orchid on his lapel every day. I was so impressed with his style of dressing that I decided to emulate him in that regard. My problem however, was that I could not afford orchids, or any part of his lifestyle, so I decided then to improve my dressing by wearing a rose in my lapel. Fortunately for me, there was a home near the entrance of Bruce Road, leading to Alrick Avenue where I lived, that grew some beautiful roses. That patch provided me a steady supply of lovely roses, which I gratefully made a part of my daily ensemble.

Over time, I came to be considered one of the best dressed men in Brent. It was with great surprise however, that I learned that there were some persons who were resentful of me and my lifestyle. Questions were asked about my ability to afford my dressing, the way I spoke and the position to which I was employed. The most surprising part, was that many of these persons were of my own colour, whom I would expect would be in proud admiration of a young black man. I was by now in my 22nd year of life, single, and enjoying myself to the fullest.

THE WAKEUP CALL

Then in November of 1960, almost two years into my job, I went to lunch as usual at midday on the last Thursday of the month. After lunch, I went to the London Astoria, where I met and danced with young ladies who came from across Continental Europe. They had come to London mainly from Sweden, France and Austria, as au pairs. They resided with English families and did various chores in return for learning to speak English. On their day-off, they would all gather for some enjoyment. And enjoyed myself I did, so much so that the afternoon passed and I had not returned to work.

I was later told that the boss had called to speak with me several times and was told on every occasion that I had gone to lunch. He called for the final time at about 4:20 pm and I was still not there. He then left a message that I should collect my employment card the next day from one of my colleagues. I was again fired from the job. This time, I was irresponsible. I was gallivanting.

I went home, calmly reflected on my reckless approach to life, and vowed never again to be fired from a job because of my behaviour. Luckily for me, a friend informed me some days later of vacancies at the place where he worked. I immediately applied for the position of storeman at the Glacier Metal Company at Ealing Road, Alperton, near Wembley. After a very brief interview, I was given the job. I was very fortunate to have obtained a job so very quickly and I thought that the Lord was watching over me.

UNIONS AT WORK AND PLAY

I started work on the sixth day of December 1960, in a department known as the Stock Product Organization. The company manufactured bearings for every type of motor vehicle, ship and airplane. The SPO was where all finished products were stocked for delivery to customers and my role was to fill the orders as they arrived.

Successful execution of the role required studying and knowing all the various items or products, makes and sizes. A test was given before confirmation. Needless to say, I was very successful in a short time. In the third week of December, I was approached by Maud Kapelle, who was the union shop steward. She informed me that this department, which employed over 150 workers, was a union shop, which meant that all the workers were members of a union. If I had any objection to being a member, I would have to seek a position in another department.

The company was the largest engineering company in England at that time, employing over 1000 workers. Some employees were located in Scotland, and had five unions including the Transport and General Workers Union, which was the one representing the department in which I was working. I had never worked at a unionised establishment before, so had no knowledge of unions or how they worked. Nevertheless, my response was a definite yes, because I did not want to have to go elsewhere. The membership fee of the

37

Transport and General Workers Union was one shilling per week. It cost an extra penny weekly to become a member of the British Labour Party. The Transport and General Workers Union had a membership of over 1.2 million workers, which meant that approximately 1.2 million pennies went to the Labour Party each week from union dues alone.

After Maud Kapelle had explained the function of the union, I became very excited about the prospect of being a member of such an organization. I was rather pleased to know that there was an organization looking after the interest of workers. I went home and told everyone what had transpired that day.

A number of my relatives and friends were already members of a union. They were happy to hear that I had now joined the fold also. I learned that members often addressed each other as 'brothers' and 'sisters', so there was a kinship which the union represented. I decided well, since I had only one sister, this was a great opportunity to extend my family. This only added to my delight at becoming a member. The events which followed my entry into the company and the union can only be described as amazing.

1961-64 will remain some of the most memorable years of my life. Those three years set the stage and laid the foundation for the things which would eventually define me. Most of those events were not previously contemplated or planned, but their reality established the platform on which my rapid and successful trade union and political life was launched. To begin, 1961 brought me into fatherhood, when in July of that year my English girlfriend gave birth to my first child, Karen and three months later, in October, my Jamaican girlfriend, who later became my wife, gave birth to my second daughter, Lavern. My lifestyle took a dramatic change. It was as if I was hit by a double whammy, but I promised myself to rise to the occasion of becoming a father.

Unfortunately, part of my intentions were shattered when I realized that the mother of my English girlfriend was racist, and did not want me to be a part of the child's life apart from paying maintenance. I therefore concentrated all my time in caring for Lavern, who we realized was sickly and needed much attention. I must confess however, that during all this,

I never stopped dancing with the Necktie Gang, which was always out on weekends, so our popularity grew with every passing day. We could be recognized on the streets collectively and singularly, and we enjoyed every moment of it, being young and energetic. The sound system operators such as Count Suckle, Duke Vin, D. Unis, Clarence, King B and Duke Henry were always eager to invite me and Needles to attend their dances to attract the dance crowd, many of whom would come to watch us perform.

We also entered dance contests at places such as Brixton Townhall and Handsworth in Birmingham and competed against popular Jamaican dancers such as Busty, Cho-Cho Mouth, Pam Pam and Satchmo. All of them had a reputation of being great in their movements on the floor, but for me, Needles was the greatest of them all.

This time, I did not let my social life negatively impact my work. My performance at the Glacier Metal Company was going great, having received a salary increase after my excellent appraisal. I was also considered the most improved worker in the department in October 1961. I had no idea that my co-workers were also appraising me, when in November, someone nominated me to contest the election for shop committee members, better known as union delegates. I had no interest in the union, other than being a member, therefore I ignored the gesture. However, someone else decided to sign my name in acceptance of the nomination, and despite my protestations, the other workers were adamant that my name should remain.

Out of a population of approximately 150 workers in the Stock Product Organization Department, only 20 were non-white, most of whom were West Indian. Among this group was an extraordinary individual by the name of Guy Elliston, who hailed from Clarendon, Jamaica. He had been elected to the shop committee the previous year. He was not an educated person per se, but was fearless, outspoken and determined and one you would be glad to have in your corner when there was a problem in the department. Strangely enough, his nickname was "Happy." Earlier that year, he had invited me to a meeting of The Willesden Friendship Council, which was one of the first race relations groups in London. It included persons such as Phil Sealy from Barbados, an Englishman by the name of Reg Freeson, Guy Elliston and yours truly, who became a member immediately on arrival that day. Reg Freeson became an elected member of the Willesden Borough Council representing the St. Raphel's Division and later became a member of parliament and Minister of Housing in Harold Wilson's government. In later years, Phil Sealy was appointed the first race relations officer in England by the government.

The meeting was held in a vacant building at Dudden Hill Lane in Willesden, which we hired from the council. Sometime later, with the council's assistance, we were able to purchase the building and named it Sir Leary Constantine Hall, after the great West Indian cricketer. Over the years, the hall became the venue for many social and political events, mainly for black residents in the surrounding area.

The company-wide election for shop committee took place in December. I abstained. At the end of the counting of votes in my department, my name registered the most votes of all candidates, thereby declaring me the winner. I became the chairman or chief union delegate of the shop committee.

Though surprised and somewhat confused, I was humbled by the overwhelming show of respect and confidence that the workers had for me in such a short time and accepted what I thought was an ordained responsibility. My new responsibilities took effect on the first day of January 1962, so I quickly went about reading all that I could on trade unions and in particular the agreements between the unions and the management, which was referred to as the bible.

The Union Workers Committee and the company's management had a policy arrangement to send new shop stewards or shop committee members on training for two weeks, without loss of pay. This training helped fast track my understanding of the trade union movement. I also soon realized that once we became delegates, especially the chief or chairman in this case, one is expected to solve issues no matter how long on the job.

My biggest surprise, however, was the discouragement from the black community in which I resided. Their remark was usually, "Leave it alone, is white people business." However this only made me more determined to succeed as the months went by. My motto was finally taking shape: "If you can't beat them, join them, learn from them, and then beat them at their own game."

To my close friends, it was an honour to be in the company of one who was elected as union representative. They also recognized that for my age and race, it was even more of a great achievement. I was later told by a female co-worker that my mannerism, the way I spoke and my attire were the three factors that propelled the workers to vote for me in such great numbers.

My sudden rise to power was echoed in many places around London, including the Jamaican High Commission, who invited me to attend a reception at their location at Bruton Street, London. There I had the great honour and privilege of meeting, Sir Lawrence Lindo, the high commissioner, who later became a good friend of mine.

But my ascendancy had just begun as the secretary of the local branch of the Transport and General Workers Union, a white man named Burt Bond, had made the decision to appoint me to represent the branch on the Wembley South Constituency Labour Party Committee, the constituency in which the company was located. My recent exposures in the few months had boosted my confidence to take on and accept any challenge presented to me, so I gladly accepted the appointment.

On the day of the constituency meeting, which was convened after working hours, I arrived with great expectation of participating in my first ever political discussion. On my arrival, I entered the room beaming with confidence and expressed my newly acquired phraseology, "Good evening Brothers!" But the reception was not at all warm or brotherly, mainly because on informing the committee secretary of my appointment, the branch secretary of the Transport and General Workers Union did not proceed to mention that I was not white.

So, the entire room which consisted of all older, white men, immediately became silent with shock, to see and hear a young black man referring to them as 'brothers.' The chairman, who sat with his glasses perched on the edge of his nose, nearly fell off his chair. It was a very uncomfortable moment for me for most of the meeting, until one member came to sit beside me and whispered, "Don't mind those old fogies, they are only surprised, that's all."

After the meeting, I conversed with this kindly, tall man, whose name was Leonard Snow. Based on his comments, I concluded that it was most unusual and unexpected to see and hear black persons being involved in politics or even trade unions at that level. The only known black person to have been involved in the political arena at that time was a Doctor David Pitt, who in 1958 /1959, ran unsuccessfully as a candidate of the Labour party in the Hampstead area of London. Ordinarily, our black brothers and sisters would only join a union because they had no choice, but taking an active part was unheard of.

Within about a year after my involvement with the union, my social activities came to a virtual stop. This transition had started with the arrival of my daughter, Lavern, in 1961. Naturally, I had to leave the home of the Pennycooks, with whom I had lived all these years and obtain accommodation for my new family with my Jamaican girlfriend. It became even more urgent by the following year as we were expecting another child, and therefore took the bold step to get married. We tied the knot in November 1962. It was a very small and private affair, because we could not afford to spend lavishly with another child on the way. Happily, my little bundle of joy, named Anita, arrived on December 4th, 1962. This added responsibility meant my dancing days were now over and I began to concentrate even more on work, the union and political matters.

At the workplace, having won all the disputes that I was involved in on behalf of the workers, my reputation as a successful and sharp union rep had spread throughout the company. By 1963, I was nicknamed "Perry Mason." Senior members of the Union Workers Committee would seek my assistance on a number of difficult cases, and as a result of this, I was selected to join the Works Committee and became a member of the all-powerful Works Council, which was a body jointly comprising a management representative and the trade unions.

I was now interacting with persons such as Lord Wilfred Brown, who was the chairman of the company, and the chairman of the Works Council;

Bill Morton, the convener of the five unions; Jack Deyael, of the Engineering Union; Burt Bond of the Transport and General Workers Union amongst other senior members and leaders of unions. I had become one of the most powerful union representatives in the company and for me, life was good.

The news of my trade union involvement and successes was spoken of beyond the boroughs of Willesden and Wembley. Black persons in those areas would stop me on the street to shake my hand with pride at my achievements. Most noticeably, though not connected, was another invitation in October 1962 from my friend, Sir Lawrence Lindo, the Jamaican high commissioner to London. He invited me to attend a reception at the Prochester Hall in Bayswater, London, in honour of Sir Alexander Bustamante and his wife Lady Bustamante on their first visit to London since their wedding. I gladly accepted.

On that occasion, I met and shook hands with Sir Alexander, John P. Gyles, Robert Lightbourne, and Donald Sangster, who was a cousin of my adopted mother and on whose knees I sat as a child in George's Valley, St. Elizabeth. I also met Oswald Harding for the first time, on that day. He would later become my good friend. After the reception, I called Sir Lawrence and thanked him for providing me the opportunity to meet with not only the leaders of my country of birth, but also all the prominent Jamaicans, whom I had never met before, who gathered for the occasion. I felt very happy to know that I was meeting with a number of persons who were community leaders in their respective areas.

I once again came to the conclusion then the Lord was guiding every step of my life. The rapid pace at which events were unfolding, and with very little encouragement from my black brothers and sisters in the first place, was almost unbelievable. I thought I was at the zenith of my ascension and would go no further, when the Transport and General Workers Union appointed me as shop steward, which authorized me to collect union dues on its behalf and for which a special credential was given.

My involvement in the Wembley South constituency meetings had also been recognized and I was invited to become a member of the Inner Circle of the group. I was also invited to attend and be a part of the discussion team along with other constituency groups from the Wembley and Willesden labour parties for the merging of the two boroughs.

The borough of Wembley at the time, was mostly conservative. Wembley South, which was a real suburban area, was represented by the conservative member of parliament, Sir Ronald Russell. The plan of the Labour Party members in both boroughs was to transform most of Wembley to the Labour Party constituencies, by moving its supporters from Willesden, which was always one of their strongholds and to bring them into Wembley. This, we hoped, would shift the balance of voting power.

My family grew again with the birth of my son in February 1964. I was filled with immense pride and joy knowing that the family name of Clarke would now likely continue for years to come. I named him Dane, after Dane Clarke my favourite actor then.

But we had outgrown our accommodation and I was forced to secure a larger dwelling. We got a house in Wembley at Cecil Avenue, which consisted of three bedrooms and a bathroom. The move to Cecil Avenue was a very delightful one. It brought me closer to my workplace and to the popular shopping area in Wembley; a few chains from the famous Wembley Stadium where all the big activities took place. There were the football finals and the popular Wembley Stadium Sunday market, where you could get all types of household articles and other products at very reasonable prices on Sundays. And, of course, Dog Racing.

The other great joy of my move was the discovery that my next door neighbour, Trevor Lewis, was also from St. Elizabeth in Jamaica. Trevor was the second son of the Jamaican politician Cleve Lewis. His younger brother Earl also resided there. I was very happy to know that I was living next door to not only a fellow Jamaican, but put colloquially, a fellow 'St. Bess' man. His older brother, Neville Lewis would visit on weekends and I struck what I considered to be a very close relationship with all three brothers. Together we went many places to include the pub, the park and even did a little betting on the horses on Saturdays.

Neville was quite adept at placing bets, and I too became attached to that particular exercise for quite a while. Needless to say, the relationship between us lasted a lifetime. On one occasion, they invited me to accompany them to meet with their father, who was the Minister of Works in Jamaica and was in England on government business. This meeting took place at the Dorchester Hotel at the west end of London. I had no political feelings about Jamaica at that time, but I was very curious to meet my friends' father whom I'd heard a lot about so I accepted the invitation and had a jolly good time.

By this time, my trade union and political activities were getting into high gear. The nickname 'Perry Mason' was playing out to be just that. I was winning all the disputes that I was asked to settle and word got out even among those who had discouraged me about getting involved in the first place. Naturally, I ignored their gestures at that stage. I felt very happy and secure in the knowledge that I had accomplished what I believed no other black person coming into England, had achieved as far as I was aware. Also, I had an unparalleled level of involvement and success in both arenas, and for that I felt very grateful. Little did I know that my peers had other plans for me.

In 1965, the merger of the two boroughs, Wembley and Willesden, gave birth to the borough of Brent. It also meant that the two trade councils; Wembley and Willesden, would automatically change and merge to form one council: The Brent Trades Council.

When I was first introduced to the term, I did not know what a trades council was. Upon doing my research, I discovered it was a body of elected delegates from all trade unions in the borough or parish, which is certified with the British Trade Union Congress. The British Trade Union Congress is the governing body of all trade unions in England, Scotland and Wales. These trade councils carried out the functions of the TUC in the local boroughs.

The local borough elections that followed that year, resulted in the Labour Party gaining control of the new borough of Brent. They immediately set about implementing their plans for the transformation of Wembley, politically. The first activity was to establish Chalk Hill Estate, a development in which houses were built to accommodate their Willesden Borough members and supporters into Wembley. To my surprise, Burt Bond, the secretary of the local branch of the Transport and General Workers Union, called me to his office to inform me that I should represent them as their delegate on this newly formed Brent Trades Council.

I accepted the appointment with the understanding that I could not continue on the Wembley South Constituency Labour Party as their representative.

Remembering my reception at my first Wembley South Constituency Labour Party meeting, I proceeded cautiously when I attended the Trades Council meeting for the first time. But the chairman on duty welcomed me warmly and wished for me an interesting experience at the council meetings. I immediately felt relaxed, despite the fact that once again, I was the only black person in the gathering.

This was the second meeting of the council. The first was convened to elect the officers and the regular meetings were to be on a monthly basis thereafter.

After the meeting, the chairman and the general secretary took me aside and explained some of the policies of the Trades Council. They also gave me documents with which I could apprise myself of the workings of the Council. I decided then and there that I would do my best to the expectations of my own convictions to rise above the odds. I knew quite a few persons who wanted and expected me to fail at this, but I was now in the big league and was determined to enjoy my time and to excel in what was then known as the local trade union powerhouse.

I contemplated that any slip-ups could reflect negatively on black people as a whole. I made it a point of duty to attend every monthly meeting and, very early in my attendance, I was placed on various local committees representing the Trades Council.

Over the years 1965 to 1969, I was placed on four different bodies, starting with the Brent Accident Prevention Committee and the Brent Local Employment Committee, which was an appointment by the Minister of Labour to oversee and report on the employment and unemployment conditions in the borough. I was placed on the Board of Governors of the Sladebrook High School and the Board of Governors of the Park Royal Hospital, all representing the Trades Council. My days and evenings were now fully occupied with very little time for pleasure.

In 1967, Navel Clarke Jnr. was welcomed into the family. Very soon after his birth, I was fortunate to secure a house from the Borough Council and we relocated back to my old stomping ground Harlesden, only this time in the Stonebridge area at 15 Denton Road.

With the information I obtained from the documents given to me by the Trades Council chairman and secretary, I decided to further my knowledge of the trade union movement. I took a one year home study course through the Transport and General Workers Union from Scotland. The study commenced in June of 1966 and was completed in May of 1967. I obtained an 86% pass mark, which qualified me for a scholarship to Ruskin College, Oxford. It was an exciting and rewarding result.

In June of 1967, the company's unions arranged a seminar for all delegates and shop committee members in Ruislip, Middlesex, not far from the workplace. The lecturer was a retired miner named Wal Hannington who, as a young man, was incarcerated for his involvement in the great hunger march on London in the year 1925. He had written several books including one entitled Mr. Chairman, which he shared with us on this occasion. Part of his speech was to encourage those of us who were not native English, and he said, "Never forget the land of your birth." An Englishman, he said, "Wherever in the world he is, he will never forget or surrender England." These words were etched in my mind as I went to bed that night and I thought of Jamaica. I took the bold step to get involved in something directly connected with my birth country.

The following week, I wrote letters to the People's National Party and the Jamaica Labour Party, the two political parties in Jamaica, requesting a copy of their Constitution and their latest manifesto. I intended to be involved in one of those parties. I first thought the Jamaica Labour Party would have been the more obvious choice, given their name, which I thought was synonymous with the Labour Party in England. I also thought they would have been the first to respond, but within two weeks after sending my letters, the only response came from the People's National Party. I received all that I requested, along with a letter from the General Secretary, a Mr. S.O. Veitch, thanking me for my interest in the People's National Party.

On reading the documents, I realized that the party's aim, objectives and policies were consistent with those of the British Labour Party, which I joined in 1960 and therefore would be a good choice for my involvement in Jamaica. The very next day I wrote back, indicating my desire to be a member and asked for a membership form to be sent to me, which they did not long after. I provided all the information requested on the document and fulfilled all the necessary requirements including sending fees for one year, after which I received an individual membership card. I was so proud of this card and the feeling that I was now linked to Jamaica. I was, however, still awaiting a response from the Jamaica Labour Party, and I unfortunately must confess that to this day, I am still waiting for that response from them.

After receiving my membership card in 1968 and showing it to almost everyone that I met, a close friend informed me of a UK based organization which was aligned to the People's National Party in Jamaica. It was known as the Jamaica Progressive League, UK and was headquartered in Clapham Common, London. I hurriedly made contact and was informed that meetings were held at 9 Gascort Road, Clapham Common on the second Sunday of each month.

Although this was quite a long distance from where I lived, I decided to join the group and participate in their activities. The gathering comprised mainly former members of the People's National Party groups and supporters in Jamaica and was chaired by Aston Hall, at whose house we met. Other persons whom I came into contact with were Cecil Collington, James Byfield, Eric McAlpine, Headley Cunningham and Theo Campbell to name a few.

The discussions at the meetings focused on current affairs in Jamaica and reminiscing on what was, back then. I was not able to speak on most of the issues that were brought forward through lack of knowledge of Jamaican politics. My position was to see how we could integrate into the British system politically and at the same time be able to assist Jamaica in whatever way we could, whether financially or through suggestions. I was in some instances very frustrated because most of the members were much older than me and I considered them to be set in their ways. Due to our age gap, I felt uneasy on a number of occasions. Despite that, however, I tried to attend meetings as regularly as possible.

DESTINY BECKONS

The transformation of my life since 1961 gave me a deep feeling of achievement as a young black man. Having broken barriers which others of my colour could not have imagined possible at that time made me consider that this was as far as I could go in the political and trade union movement, but I was once again ever so wrong in my thinking.

In October 1968, I arrived home from work and found a lot of sealed parcels and other articles such as typewriters, Gestetner, stationery, ink and table in my wife's sewing room. They belonged to the Trades Council. There was also a note saying that the general secretary of the council had family problems in Wales and had to return urgently. It went on to state that I was selected to act as secretary until the next annual general meeting in February of 1969.

I felt that this time, someone was playing a prank on me. With no consultation or questions asked, this time they had gone too far. I immediately called the Chairman, Ken Spence who by then had become a very close friend and enquired about what was taking place. Was this some kind of setup? He stated that it was the unanimous decision of the members of the council that I was considered the most suitable person to act on such short notice, therefore I should just give it a try. With some reluctance, I accepted the challenge.

At the next monthly meeting, I entered the hall as nervous as a kitten, having to write from memory, the minutes of the last meeting. I was worried that it would not capture most of the salient points that were raised and discussed. But to my great delight, I was given a cheerful welcome at my first sitting at the head table and after reading the minutes, I was congratulated on presenting one of the best minutes for a long time. I was so overjoyed; it was as if the world had been lifted off my shoulders. From then on my confidence grew, with Ken Spence, head of the Union at the United Dairies in Cricklewood, guiding me all the way.

The ensuing months leading up to February 1969 were used to understand and perform the role of secretary, mainly to avoid embarrassment before handing over to the incoming person who would be the next secretary. In addition to preparing the agenda which had the report, I was expected to present a financial report and budget for the next year. This I did with the assistance of the chairman. Everything was ready for the final day of my role as acting general secretary, which was scheduled for the last Wednesday in the month of February 1969. I had positive expectations for the outcome, and speaking of expectations, on the home front, my darling wife announced that we were again expecting an addition to the family. Perhaps for the first time, this announcement found me completely relaxed and ready. Our current home could accommodate the family growth, we were doing well financially and our lives were fulfilled and happy. This time, we were much more prepared for our new born.

The Trades Council meetings were held in a building they now owned through succession when Willesden Trades and Labour Hall converged to form the borough of Brent in 1965. It was located on Willesden High Street, NW10. The annual general meeting was surprisingly fully supported with all delegates in attendance. Some of the faces were not seen for months, which indicated the importance they placed on this event. I was given a warm welcome as I entered the hall, which I believe was an expression of thanks for my efforts over the short period and having taken my seat on the platform beside the chairman, an almost immediate silence emerged.

The chairman pounded the gavel and declared the meeting should come to order with prayer, welcome and opening remarks. He then called upon me to present the report and budget to the members. After my presentation and a few questions asked, a vote of approval was given, which made me the happiest person. I rose again to thank them for the support I was given, especially from Ken Spence and a few others and further pledged my full support to the incoming secretary.

Election of officers saw the chairman being re-elected for the third time and then it was time for the nominations for the general secretary. A delegate by the name of Peter Papps, who was one of the bright and outspoken delegates of the council, rose and begged to nominate Brother Navel (Neville) Clarke, as I was referred to then, for the position of general secretary. Tom Durkin, another delegate who everyone knew as a registered member of the Communist Party in Brent and in England for that matter, seconded the motion.

The chairman's call for "Any other nomination?" was met with a resounding "NO!" on three occasions. "What the hell is happening here?" I thought. Suddenly a feeling of numbness overcame my body. I started crying and shivering, I could not believe that this was happening to me.

In all my working life, I have never applied for or campaigned for a promotion, yet I was always being propelled into one leadership position or another. Even so, this was unthinkable. There was a standing ovation after the chairman's declaration, and many delegates came to shake my hand and pat me on the back in congratulation.

After the meeting, Ken and a few other members escorted me to The Crown, which was a nearby pub, located across from the bus garage in Willesden High Road. Their intention was for us to have a celebratory drink, but that lasted a couple of hours instead. After the first round, all I wanted to do was hurry home to share the events that had unfolded with my wife and kids. When I finally got there, my wife was already asleep, but I could not wait until the next morning to relieve myself of the pressure that had built up in me. Even then, I still could not believe what had taken place earlier that evening. I woke her up and said, "Guess what has happened?" "What!" she responded with a sudden shock, as if something deadly had taken place. I began to explain to her as calmly as I could, given my state of mind, the events of the evening.

A kiss on the lips and a congratulatory hug was my reward.

The next morning, I went to work and met with the Transport and General Workers Union Branch Secretary, Burt Bond, and the company's Union Convenor, Bill Morton to inform them of the result of the election, which was received with great delight. According to Morton, he was not surprised by my election to the post of secretary, because it was something he thought I deserved and he had envisaged my rise to high positions in the trade union and political arena. It also meant greater recognition for the union in the company, because I was their delegate to the Trades Council.

The news of my ascendency was met with jubilation in my department SPO, with hugs and kisses from the ladies and handshakes from the men, all of whom were responsible for my entrance into the trade union activities in the first place. The emotions that followed from this reception brought tears in abundance.

The chairman of the council, Ken Spence, had volunteered to do a press release of my appointment and to officially inform the TUC, which was then headed by none other than the famous Victor Feather. The TUC was the governing body of the Trades Council from which the stamp of approval and the issuance of my credentials for the performing of the duties on its behalf would be given.

I received my official stamp and credentials one week later along with other printed paraphernalia explaining the work and responsibility of the secretary of the Trades Council. These, along with the authority of the TUC, automatically made me one of the most powerful persons in the borough of Brent. This was a historic event, as further research would reveal that I was the first black person in British history to be elected head or secretary of a trade union organization.

What this meant to me, was that all eyes were now focused on me from every conceivable quarter, especially from the white population, not only in Brent, but in other boroughs. The Labour Party members of parliament, councillors, trade union members and their families by extension, numbering approximately 45,000 strong comprised the pillars on which the Trades Council rested.

I was now convinced that destiny had chosen this young black man to be a pioneer in the advancement of non-white people in England into the trade union and political arena which was the ultimate bastion of power for the working classes at the time. In a very short time I became aware of the enormity of the responsibility and the extent of the role of the secretary, in that, I now had to meet and interact with local leaders, not delegates of the trade unions but members of parliament, mayors, chief of police, Trades Council secretaries from other boroughs in London and outside of London. It became necessary and urgent upon my taking office to be involved in the vigorous and combative debate against the then government's intention in January of 1969, to curb the powers of the trade unions by the presentation to parliament and the subsequent publication by Barbara Castle, the first secretary of state for employment and productivity. The proposed legislation entitled "In Place of Strife, a Policy for Industrial Relations," which ignited a fire that spread across the entire British trade union movement.

It was therefore my responsibility to galvanize the Union members in the borough of Brent in the demonstration against the Bill, in solidarity with the rest of London and beyond. My call to action was met with great enthusiasm, resulting in several planning meetings and the involvement of many volunteers.

It attracted persons such as John Butta of the Teachers Association, Jack Dromey, Harriet Harmon who later became a MP, Winchester James, a great Jamaican trade unionist, and Tom Durkin to name a few. What they all had in common, was they were good friends of mine, to whom I delegated several responsibilities to assist in making this demonstration a success.

The workers and their unions became very angry with the Labour Party government for the introduction of this Bill and lobbied members of parliament for its withdrawal. Their anger, in my view, was so deep that it contributed to the Labour Party losing the control of the borough of Brent in the local elections of June 1969. It meant also that the former borough of Willesden was now controlled by the conservatives for the first time in thirty years and I wondered if my success in the galvanizing of the people played a part in that outcome.

THE NEW HORIZON

June 1969 was indeed an eventful time in my life. Firstly, with the borough now being controlled by the conservatives, I had to interact on behalf of the union with some of the new councillors, and in particular with Ruby Taylor, the new mayor with whom it was important to have established a good working relationship. Fortunately, in a short while that relationship grew exceptionally well, and very friendly.

Just around that time, the Brent Teachers' Association, which was one of the largest groups in the Trades Council had their Annual General Meeting and had elected new officers to include those who would serve on the Trades Council. I anticipated welcoming them at the next meeting of the council, but surprisingly one evening I arrived home and was about to have a hearty meal when I heard a knock on the front door. My wife, who is a light-skinned or fair Jamaican lady, answered the door.

On doing so, she saw an Englishman who with some surprise, looked at her and said, "Oh, I'm sorry, I'm looking for a Mr. Clarke and this address was given as his residence." Her reply was "Yes, this is Mr. Clarke's residence. He is my husband." He then responded, "The secretary of the Brent Trades Council. Are you sure?" My wife then replied, "Yes I'm sure that he is my husband and the position he holds is secretary of the Brent Trades Council." With that, she said "Would you care to come in?" "He is just about to have his dinner, but he won't be long." At this, he entered the house and was asked to wait in the living room. He was offered the customary cup of tea, which he declined.

After my meal, I entered the living room and the gentleman stood up and asked me, "Are you Mr. Clarke of the Brent Trades Council?" "Yes sir, the very same" "How can I help you?" I replied. He then introduced himself as the newly elected treasurer and delegate to the Trades Council from the Brent Teachers' Association. He went on to add that he had brought the affiliation fees since he lived fairly nearby and wanted ever-so-much to meet the secretary of the Trades Council. I wondered why he couldn't have waited for the next meeting of the council to hand over the cheque.

As we took our seats, he proceeded to ask questions about the trade union movement as if to test my knowledge and was noticeably surprised when I answered his questions. Then, to my surprise, he suddenly shifted the discussion to the doctrine of Karl Marx. I informed him that I had read Karl Marx, but found that most of his theories were just that, and not workable, so it was not worth the discussions going forward. After a few more minutes on local issues, he handed me an envelope with a cheque and bade me good night.

After his departure, I sat and calmly considered what had transpired in that brief meeting. The stark reality of the racial undercurrent was brought to my face in my living room. Here was a white man, and a teacher to boot, who undoubtedly was convinced that a black man would be incapable of holding such a high and powerful position, simply because of the colour of his skin. I wondered, what was he teaching the children in his school?

Since my involvement in the trade union movement and politics, beginning in 1960, this was my first encounter with this blatant level of white supremacy and it made me upset. "This cannot be happening to me," I thought. I was even more determined to rise and fulfil my motto, "If you can't beat them, join them, learn from them and beat them at their own game." Interestingly, however, as the months and years passed, the gentleman became my closest ally and friend inside and outside of the Trades Council. My next eventful moment in the month of June, was the evening that I arrived home and my wife handed me an envelope addressed to me from someone by the name of Michael Manley from Jamaica. I said to her, "I know Norman Washington Manley, but not Michael Manley."

With some curiosity, I opened the envelope and slowly read its contents. As I read the document for the third time, I suddenly realized that as a result of me becoming a member of the People's National Party in Jamaica two years before, my name must have appeared on their register, hence the contact. The letter was dated June 14, 1969 and it served to inform me that Mr. Michael Manley was the newly elected leader of the People's National Party and the Opposition Leader in Jamaica. It further stated that he would be visiting a number of countries in the months of September and October, the first of which would be England, later that year. He requested that I be involved in the planning of that visit.

Immediately I thought, "How could this goodly gentleman, who I had neither met nor heard of before, believe that I was capable of undertaking such a venture?" It took me a few days of wondering and pondering if I should, or if I could before I finally decided it was my chance to do something for the country of my birth.

As a result of my position as general secretary of the Trades Council, I had all the necessary tools to respond to Mr. Michael Manley. I went to the typewriter, confirmed that it had carbon paper, and courageously proceeded to reply to him. With one finger stabbing at each letter on the keyboard, I informed him of my willingness to carry out his request. It took a little while to complete as it was my first time typing, but I would not be deterred. I wanted him to be assured that notwithstanding the fact that I had never met him, I was willing to carry out the task. At the end, I had a letter that was respectable. Thank God.

In his letter, Mr. Manley had stated that he would like to meet as many Jamaicans as possible on his visit to England. He wanted to motivate them to help their homeland while abroad and to interest those going to school or who have learned new skills to return home and help the country progress in the coming years.

With this in mind, I approached the one person who could assist me to fulfil my task without any hesitation. He was also the most popular person that I knew, plus he was attached to the Jamaican High Commission. I went to my good friend, Cecil Collier, who just as I knew he would, gladly agreed to help prepare the programme and put all the necessary materials together.

One week after, I received a letter from one Tom McNally, overseas secretary of the British Labour Party, advising me that Mr. Manley had asked him to assist with the arrangements for the visit. My team was now beginning to take shape and we were meeting on a regular basis to make our plans. I kept Mr. Manley informed of our plans and progress at every stage.

The team kept in constant contact with Jamaicans in various parts of London. Special effort was made to ensure members of the Progressive League UK and the Association of Jamaicans UK were informed, reminded and re-reminded of the visit. The big event was scheduled for September 20th. Discovering that Mr. Manley was also a trade unionist in Jamaica increased my desire for him to have a successful visit. I therefore decided to involve my fellow trade union leaders in the planning, in the hope that they would also meet with Mr. Manley.

With the knowledge that I was chosen to spearhead this important event, not for an organization or borough or parish, but the country of Jamaica, made me the proudest man living in London at the time and so with boastful exuberance I went to my workplace and made the announcement. First to the secretary of the TSWU branch, Burt Bond and to the convenor of the Unions in the company, Mr. Bill Morton and then to my workmates in the SPO department, which I had worked for many years.

There were quite a number of Jamaicans working in the Glacier Metal Company, so in keeping with Mr. Manley's request, I asked the two leaders to arrange for Mr. Manley to visit the company and meet with them. They agreed.

Mr. Morton also suggested that I should ask the chairman of the company to meet with Mr. Manley, who he described as the future leader of Jamaica. A tour of the plant was also suggested as something I should propose. I was pleasantly surprised with the suggestions, which had not entered my mind. The chairman, who would normally preside over the meeting of the Company's Works Council, was a close acquaintance, since I was also a member of the council. So occasionally when he attended, we would be there together. Thankfully, the chairman agreed to meet with Mr. Manley.

Mr. Manley's visit was scheduled to commence Saturday, 20th through to the 23rd. I arranged the visit to my company for Monday, the 22nd so it would coincide with Jamaicans being at work. At this time, he would also meet with the Union bosses. The tour was to start at 10 am sharp. The chairman had postponed his board meeting, scheduled for that day, for one hour, so he could meet and walk with Mr. Manley.

The overall programme included a meeting with the Progressive League UK, at 10 am on Saturday at Gascart Road in Clapham Common. Later in the afternoon, at 3 pm, a reception would be held at the Commonwealth Institute in Regents Park, followed by a meeting with Jamaican nationals at the Anson Hall in Cricklewood in the borough of Brent. This was scheduled for 8 pm. Sunday, the 21st had no scheduled activities so Mr. Manley could use that day for his private business and relaxation. Monday and Tuesday, the 22nd and 23rd respectively were days scheduled for the visit to Glacier, a meeting with the Association of Jamaicans and a meeting with students at the West Indian Standing Conference in Earl's Court. All this information was sent to Mr. Manley, prior to his arrival, which he approved.

While the plans were being worked out and the scheduling was underway, concerns about the budget began to arise at the Trades Council. We became concerned that with the increased activities of the Council and my ambitious budget and the current financial position, we would not be able to meet our objectives. An immediate solution was to increase affiliation fees from one penny per member from each branch or association to two pennies. As secretary, this task fell on me and as a long term solution, I convinced my officers to approve the rental of the ground floor of the building to my good friend Jeffery Palmer, who transformed that space into a night club, which was later named the Apollo Club. This venture was a significant turning point in the fortunes of the Trades Council, and in a very short while we were able to meet all our expenses and build up a healthy financial account.

With our domestic affairs in order, we now needed to turn our attention to a pressing matter, which if passed into law, could overthrow all we had worked for as a body to defend the rights of workers. To begin, our most urgent task then was to mobilize the unions in Brent into pressuring the government to withdraw the white paper titled, "In Place of Strife," which was presented by Barbara Castle, the Minister of Labour in January 1968. Its contents objectively presented a serious threat to the very existence of the trade union movement. After agitation and the threats of withdrawal of support to the Labour Party, the Harold Wilson government put the matter on hold.

Unfortunately, the Conservative Government, led by Edward Heath, won the general election in 1969 and wasted no time in introducing their version of "In Place of Strife," now called the Industrial Relations Bill, which imposed even greater restriction on the unions. This version of the Bill contained a programme of curbing the union's power by introducing hefty fines or imprisonment on the trade unions and their members who participated in what they termed as 'unofficial' or 'sympathy' strikes. To this, the Trade Councils were instructed by the secretary of the TUC, Victor Feather to intensify the mobilization of the membership to 'Kill the Bill.'

It became the rallying cry for all unions to 'Kill the Bill.' Trades Councils throughout England were called upon to support the call to 'Kill the Bill' and as secretary of the Trades Council, it was my responsibility to organize the unions in the borough of Brent to participate in the several meetings and other activities arising there from. I immediately set about making preparations which included creating the Brent Trades Council's banner in readiness for the demonstration against the Bill.

My first duty was to attend a mass meeting in Croydon, Ruskin House, along with selected members to make plans for a demonstration and then to visit the House of Commons to lobby our respective members of parliament to vote against the bill.

The meeting took place on a bitterly cold day in January, when we met to strategize the plans for the demonstration. Trade unionists from as far as Scotland were in attendance. My close colleague and fellow union representative, Winchester James, a former delegate of the National Workers Union in Jamaica at J. Wray and Nephew, was always by my side and together, we travelled by coach to Westminster to lobby our MP, Laurie Pavitt.

On arrival, we headed straight to the bathroom, having consumed several pints of beer to combat the effects of the weather whilst in Croydon. We returned to the outside of the House of Commons, and none of our colleagues from Brent were to be found. We then decided to enter the building with another group, who we were told were miners. However, we were the only black faces around, which made us very conspicuous indeed. Apparently, it was quite unusual for black persons to be involved in trade union activities at that level.

Upon entering the building, Jimmy and I stopped for a while to admire the architecture and ambience in the House of Commons, but our newfound colleagues had proceeded to their MPs' chambers. We were now stranded, and did not know where to go. We were also unaware of the fact that an inspector of police had taken a keen interest in our presence and followed us inside. Having observed our dilemma, he came to us and remarked, "I thought you weren't with that lot." Realizing that we were now in a pickle, I said to him, "How could you tell? We are coal miners who didn't bother to wash off." He laughed and then said to us, "I will have to ask you to accompany me outside." Then I thought, "what a shame, all this excitement of entering the House of Commons one day, only to be thrown out on my very first occasion." I would have to wait on the upcoming activities to be an active participant. Back home I went, to continue planning for Mr. Manley's visit as well as the arrival of the newest members of my own household.

On the morning of August 1, 1969, the midwife was called to assist in the delivery of our baby. A veteran at this by now, I sat calmly in the living room awaiting the arrival. I suddenly heard the cry of a new born baby, which made me very happy. The midwife then called to me and said, 'Mr. Clarke, would you kindly call the doctor, there is another baby on the way.' I guess I was bowled over by that news as the next thing I knew, the midwife was slapping me on the cheek saying "Wake up Mr. Clarke, the other one has arrived." "Twins?" "No one in my family ever expected twins." I said. Well, you got a girl and a boy, be happy," was her reply.

We named this twin bundle of joy Paula, who arrived first, and Rodney, the boy who I hoped terminated reproduction in the marriage.

The month went by very quickly and September was up on us. Preparations for Mr. Manley's visit were in high gear. Invitations were sent to prominent Jamaicans, officials of the British Labour Party, The Liberal Party and indeed the Conservative Party. Members of the Jamaican High Commission, in particular, were extended invitations in gratitude for their assistance in the preparations for the reception at The Commonwealth Institute, which would take place on September 20th. All other planned engagements were confirmed and ready to go.

Navel Clarke

**LOOKING DAPPER IN 3 PIECE SUIT
AND TIE AND A ROSE BUD**

Rocky Pennycook

MEMBER OF THE NECKTIE GANG

Some members of
'The Necktie Gang'

L-R: DARREL BLACKWOOD, DUDLEY MCBEAN, NAVEL CLARKE

ID Cards – Worker's Union

POWER & ENGINEERING

Newspaper tribute at the passing of Wal Hannington,

TRADE UNION LECTURER

loc

MINISTRY OF LABOUR
LONDON AND SOUTH EASTERN REGIONAL OFFICE
Hanway House, Red Lion Square, LONDON W.C.1
Telegrams: Divex, Phone, London
Telephone: HOLborn 8454, *ext.* 188

Your reference:
Our reference: A.152/65

14 July 1966.

Dear Sir,

I am glad to be able to inform you that your
nomination by The Brent Trades Council to serve on the
Workpeople's Panel of the Willesden and Wembley Local
Employment Committee has been accepted and, on behalf of
the Minister of Labour, I have much pleasure in formally
appointing you a member of the Committee. The appointment
is for the period ending 18th January 1969, unless
previously terminated by the Minister.

I am enclosing for your information a memorandum on
the constitution and functions of Local Employment
Committee (L E C 5/9) and leaflets on travelling,
subsistence and lost time allowances (A/cs 150 and
A/cs 152).

Will you kindly confirm as soon as possible your
willingness to accept the appointment. A post free label
is enclosed for this purpose.

The Manager of the Willesden Employment Exchange,
Mr. R.J. Harrison, who is Secretary to the Committee, will
then send you in due course the usual notices of meetings.

Yours faithfully,

P. N. RUSSELL
for Regional Controller

N. Clarke, Esq.,
64 Cecil Avenue,
WEMBLEY,
Middlesex.

Appointment to serve on

Workpeople's Panel

OF THE WILLESDEN & WEMBLEY EMPLOYMENT COMMITTEE

TRANSPORT & GENERAL WORKERS UNION

REGISTERED TRADE UNION No 1824T.

REGISTERED OFFICES
Transport House, Smith Square
WESTMINSTER
LONDON, S.W.1

General Secretary:
FRANK COUSINS

CHIEF OFFICE
COMMUNICATION

Asst. Gen. Secretary:
H. R. NICHOLAS, O.B.E.
Asst. Executive Secretary:
J. L. JONES, M.B.E.

AJC/DS/FL.24A

13th July, 1967.

Mr. N.F. Clarke,
25, Clenton Road,
Stonebridge,
London N.W.9.

Dear Brother Clarke,

THE UNION'S HOME STUDY COURSE

I am pleased to return your final set of material on completion of this course. Your average marking over the whole course is ___86.0___ % Your tutor's comments on your test papers are as follows:-

An encouraging level of performance. On papers 1 and 3 you achieved very good marks.

In view of the standard you have attained on Stage One, you are eligible to apply to make an attempt to gain a certificate. Please let me know if you wish to apply, at the same time giving me the date you are ready to start work. For Stage Two you are asked to give written answers to set questions, and the material for these is all contained in the booklets you have already received.

In any case I would like to take this opportunity of congratulating you on your industry and determination in completing Stage One, and I am sure you have benefited from the time and effort you have put into your studies. No doubt too you will find the booklets, notes and answers useful for future reference.

Please help bring this unique home study course to the notice of other members who may be interested. Two forms are enclosed for this purpose. Publicity material describing other educational facilities open to you is also enclosed, and I look forward to hearing from you again.

With best wishes,

Yours fraternally,

Tony Corfield.

Secretary,
Education Department

Positive results from the
Union's Home Study Course

71

THE GLACIER METAL COMPANY LIMITED

ALPERTON WEMBLEY MIDDLESEX ENGLAND

Telegrams and Cables: GLAMET, WEMBLEY. (Telex No. 22729)
Telephone: 997 6611 (25 lines) S.T.D. (outside London) 01-997 6611

EUROPE'S LARGEST MANUFACTURERS OF PLAIN BEARINGS

OUR REF. PD/RGM/CW   YOUR REF.
EXT. No.

27th October, 1967

TO WHOM IT MAY CONCERN

Navel Foster Clarke has been employed by
the Company since 5th December 1960, in our
Warehouse.   During this time he has more than
proved himself to be a reliable and conscientious
member and this has enabled him to command payment
at the end of his wage bracket.

In addition Mr. Clarke has played an active
and useful part in the represtative system of the
Company and has shown himself to be a clear and
constructive thinker.

For and on behalf of
GLACIER METAL COMPANY LIMITED

R. G. Montagu
Headquarters Personnel Officer

THE ASSOCIATED ENGINEERING GROUP

*Recommendation Letter from
Glacier Metal Company*

PEOPLE'S NATIONAL PARTY
INDIVIDUAL MEMBERSHIP
Subscription Card

Constituency...... "OVERSEAS"

This is to certify that

Name "COMRADE" NAVEL FOSTER CLARKE

Address LONDON, N.W. 10, ENGLAND

has paid up subscription for the period...............

COVERING DUES FOR 19 1968

Secretary.................

Dated 24/4/68

Individual Membership Card

PEOPLE'S NATIONAL PARTY (JAMAICA)

IN PLACE OF STRIFE

A POLICY FOR INDUSTRIAL RELATIONS

Presented to Parliament by the First Secretary of State and
Secretary of State for Employment and Productivity
by Command of Her Majesty
January 1969

LONDON
HER MAJESTY'S STATIONERY OFFICE
3s. 6d. net

Cmnd. 3888

CONTENTS

IN PLACE OF STRIFE

A POLICY FOR INDUSTRIAL RELATIONS

1. There are necessarily conflicts of interest in industry. The objective of our industrial relations system should be to direct the forces producing conflict towards constructive ends. This can be done by the right kind of action by management, unions and Government itself. This White Paper sets out what needs to be done.

2. Our present system of industrial relations has substantial achievements to its credit, but it also has serious defects. It has failed to prevent injustice, disruption of work and inefficient use of manpower. It perpetuates the existence of groups of employees who, as the result of the weakness of their bargaining position, fall behind in the struggle to obtain their full share of the benefits of an advanced industrial economy. In other cases management and employees are able unfairly to exploit the consumer and endanger economic prosperity. It has produced a growing number of lightning strikes and contributed little to increasing efficiency. There are still areas of industry without any machinery for collective bargaining at all. Radical changes are needed in our system of industrial relations to meet the needs of a period of rapid technical and industrial change.

3. Until action is taken to remedy these defects, conflict in British industry will often be damaging and anti-social. The Government places the following proposals before Parliament and the nation convinced that they are justified on two main grounds. First, they will help to contain the destructive expression of industrial conflict and to encourage a more equitable, ordered and efficient system, which will benefit both those involved and the community at large. Second, they are based on the belief that the efforts of employers, unions and employees to reform collective bargaining need the active support and intervention of Government.

4. The reasons for the first of these propositions must emerge as the Government's proposals are stated and explained in turn. But there is need, at the outset, to say something about the past and future role of Government in this field.

THE ROLE OF GOVERNMENT IN INDUSTRIAL RELATIONS

5. The State has always been involved in the process of industrial relations. It has always had to provide a framework of law for dealing with the activities of individuals and groups struggling to advance and protect their interests. The growth of employer power in the 19th century challenged the adequacy of the conventional doctrine of "laissez-faire" and highlighted the need for employees to combine in their own defence. The result was the growth of trade unions and contributed little to examine how far the law should tolerate "coercive" action in "restraint of trade" by employers or trade unions and how far it should seek to defend the wider interests of the community. In the ensuing debate on the principles to be applied, two conflicting philosophies emerged in reports of successive Royal

Excerpt from White Paper,
"IN PLACE OF STRIFE"

74

HOUSE OF COMMONS
LONDON. SW1

8th May, 1969.

Dear Brother Clarke,

Thank you for your letter. I am conscious of the concern felt by you and your colleagues, and by other trade unionists. I think it fair to say that not all the protesters have gone deeply into the provisions of the White Paper. I enclose a copy of Barbara Castle's speech which gives her side of the case, together with another comment which you might find of interest.

It should be realised that the basic objective of the White Paper is to make collective bargaining obligatory upon the employer, and the conciliation proposals mean that whatever the cause of the dispute this has to be removed immediately by the employer pending proper agreement. In other words, the reason for the strike must immediately be removed.

However, like, you, I shall watch with interest the special conference of the T.U.C. on June 5th, and the present negotiations between the Government and the T.U.C. I know you would wish me to be objective on the Government's proposals, but I cannot do this until the Bill is published and its contents known. But as your members know, on most matters where I have differed from the Government, whatever action I have taken I have done in the light of what I considered best both for the Labour and Trade Union Movements in which I have spent my lifetime.

Yours fraternally,

Laurie Pavitt

N. F. Clarke, Esq.,
The Brent Trade Council,
15. Denton Road.
N.W.10.

Letter from Laurie Pavitt, MP, UK

EARLY COMMENTARY ON MATTERS OF INTEREST REGARDING WHITE PAPER

HOUSE OF COMMONS
LONDON. SW1

7th May 1969.

Mr. N.P. Clarke,
Secretary,
Brent Trades Council,
15 Denton Road,
Stonebridge,
N.W.10.

Dear Mr. Clarke,

Thank you for your letter of May 5 regarding the White Paper "In place of strife". I regret that the views of the Brent Trades Council which it contains should reflect so much misunderstanding of the content of the White Paper.

Whatever reservations there may be regarding the proposals about secret pre-strike ballots, conciliation pauses and unconstitutional strikes, I welcome the Government's document, both as a trade unionist and as a socialist – for the reasons briefly summarised in my February 3 political circular letter "Charter for Trade Union Advance".

As I indicated then, I hope and believe that the trade union movement can deal with the three issues of dispute without the need for statutory powers to be invoked. Several unions have already done so – the N.U.M., Boilermakers, E.T.U., A.E.F., T.G.W.U. among them – in various ways.

What is more, the features which the T.U.C. have warmly welcomed overwhelmingly predominate in the White Paper. They comprise 24 out of the 27 proposals – many for which we have been fighting for years in the Labour Movement. The legislation proposed will strengthen trade unionism enormously.

Holding these views, I will naturally vote for such legislation; but I will do my best to get those issues which cause anxiety dealt with through the T.U.C. rather than by statutory powers. I know that this is what the Labour Government wants, despite misrepresentation and misunderstanding about the White Paper. Both Harold Wilson and Barbara Castle have made this clear; and I hope that such alternative methods will result from the talks now going on between the Government and the T.U.C. and the special Congress in June.

Meanwhile, I repeat previous invitations to you and your colleagues – that I would be glad to come along to a meeting to hear your views on this subject, and on other aspects of Government policy, and to express my own. You are welcome to ring me on Abbey 7000, extension 1321.

I am also hoping to arrange a meeting at the House of Commons later this month, to discuss the White Paper, and hope that you and your officers will be able to attend.

Yours sincerely,

R. Freeson

Reg Freeson, M.P.

Letter from Reg Freeson, (M.P. UK)

**INVITING MEMBERS OF THE TRADE UNIONS COUNCIL TO
A MEETING TO DISCUSS ASPECTS OF THE WHITE PAPER**

No._____

25 South Camp Road,
Kingston 16,
June 14, 1969.

Mr. N.F. Clarke,
15 Denton Road,
Stonebridge,
London N.W.10.

Dear Sir,

This is to advise you that I will be visiting England
as Leader of the Opposition starting on Saturday, September 20.

I will be available for meetings and functions in the
U.K. on Saturday September 20, Sunday 21, Monday 22 and Tuesday 23.

My visit to England is the first leg of an official tour
which will be taking me to England, Africa, Canada and the United
States.

I am inviting your active participation in the planning
and execution of this very important trip.

The purpose of the tour is to meet Jamaicans abroad,
migrant workers, students and Jamaicans who are permanent settlers
in the various countries.

Firstly, to report on the PNP and the state of the country,
and to interest them to help their home-land while abroad and to
interest them in returning home.

Secondly, to revive and reactivate a PNP organisation in
the UK. For students; to discover how they are getting on, what
help they would need from the Jamaican Government, and to impress on
them the absolute necessity of returning home when their studies are
completed in order to give their country the benefit of their
training. I would also want to discover what conditions they think
would induce them to return home.

I also propose to meet groups of other nationals interested
in Jamaica and able to help us, to tell them of the best ways in which
their help could be channeled, and of our needs.

I would like you to help me by arranging to meet other
leaders in your area so as to plan my activities while there, and to
ensure that I meet as many Jamaicans and West Indians as possible.

I would appreciate your writing to me immediately on
receipt of this letter, letting me know what you propose doing and
keeping me advised of your progress as time goes on. You might also
let me have any ideas you might have that might make the visit to
your area mutually beneficial.

I look forward to hearing from you and thank you in advance
for all you will do to make my tour a success.

Yours sincerely,

....

Michael Manley,
President, People's National Party
and Leader of the Opposition.

First letter from
Mr. Michael Manley, (PNP, Ja)

OUTLINING HIS PLANS TO TOUR THE DIASPORA TO GARNER SUPPORT
FOR HIS COUNTRY AND PARTY AND REQUESTING MY HELP FOR THE UK LEG

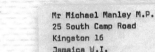

Mr Michael Manley M.P.   9 July 69
25 South Camp Road
Kingston 16
Jamaica W.I.

Dear Mr Manley

Thanks for your letter of 16th June informing me of your intended
visit to England in September, and giving me an opportunity to
participate in the planning of your trip.

I would first like to apologise for the delay in answering your
letter, but due to unforseen developments in this matter I was unable
to do so before now.

Since receiving your letter I have met three other persons who have
received similar letters from you, which has put us in a rather difficult
situation in planning a programme for our respective areas, as we
have the thought that you might have written to others who might be
planning programmes for the same time as we are.

It is felt that this might add chaos instead of success to your trip.

My proposals were that in my area which is Brent, one of the largest
boroughs in London consisting of the largest Jamaican community, which
has never had the opportunity to welcome and hear one of their leaders
we would like to invite you to speak at a mass meeting of Jamaicans and
other West Indians on Sunday 21st. We would also arrange for you to
visit one of the largest engineering combines in the country, The
Glacier Metal Company, a member of the Associated Engineering Group,
on Monday 22nd. The purpose of this visit to Glacier would be to
see fellow Jamaicans at work, to discuss their skills, to meet the
Trade Union body and be their guest, to meet with management and other
personnel to discuss industrial and race relations throughout the
company.

Unfortunately, I have not had the opportunity to discuss my proposals
with the other letter holders before informing you of the situation.

I would like to suggest that you get in contact with one reliable
person and send him or her the names of all the people that you have
written to, so that they may meet and co-ordinate a programme which
would be adequate to all concerned, details of which would be
communicated to you as soon as possible.

I also fear that there are many who might use your visit as a means
to exploit their fellow countrymen by advertising dances in your name.

I have also met members of the Jamaican Progressive League who are deeply
concerned about the whole affair.

I sincerely hope that this suggestion will be accepted and that Jamaicans
in Brent will get the opportunity to meet and hear the next Prime
Minister of their country.

May I take this opportunity to wish you all success in your future
ventures and hoping to hear from you very soon.

Yours fraternally

My response to
Mr. Michael Manley, (PNP. Ja)
INDICATING MY COMMITMENT TO ASSIST, AND INITIAL THOUGHTS

22nd August, 1969.

Dear Mr. Clarke,

        We have been asked to arrange a visit
to this country by Mr. Michael Manley, Leader of
the Opposition and Leader of the Peoples' National
Party of Jamaica from September 20th-23rd. He has
asked for arrangements to be made to enable him to
meet representatives of the Jamaican community
in Britain. If it is convenient to you, I would
suggest a joint meeting of representatives in London
on Sunday, September 21st. I would be grateful if
you would be kind enough to reply as soon as possible so that arrangements for such a meeting can
be made.

        Yours sincerely,

        Tom McNally
        Overseas Secretary.

        (Signed in Mr.McNally's absence)

N.F. Clarke, Esq.,
15, Denton Road,
Stonebridge,
LONDON, N.W.10.

Letter from Tom McNally,
(Overseas Secretary, Labour Party, UK)

INSTRUMENTAL MEMBER OF THE MICHAEL MANLEY UK TOUR PLANNING COMMITTEE

"Kill the Bill" March protesters came out in their numbers

"Kill the Bill" March protesters with posters

The Great March

Sunday February 21st, 1971. A remarkable day in British history. The people came out on to the streets of London in their tens of thousands to protest.

Ordinary people. Like you and me, as they say. Veterans of pre-war marches of the unemployed, some of them. But more who had never dreamed of demonstrating. For many of them politics was a game played by others, while they got on with the work.

But now the politicians had gone too far. The time had come to say 'No' to a Bill designed to strengthen the power of their employers and weaken the hands of their unions.

From all parts of London they came. From all parts of Britain. On 34 special trains and two special planes. And 230 special buses. In cars, by bike, on foot and by bus or by tube.

Mining families from close-knit villages, white collar workers and their wives from red-brick suburbs, the cheerful coteries of men who know the unique comradeship of going to work every day while it's still dark, the laughing girls who make cloth in antique mills or the clothes of today in yesterday's workshops, the quiet farmworkers in their Sunday-best suits, the restless men from Britain's neglected areas where jobs are getting scarcer and scarcer. Thousand upon thousand upon thousand of them. Seven miles of people, ten to fifteen abreast.

And with them came the bands they had built up themselves and heard and helped in rehearsal, and the banners newly painted, or treasured works of popular art that had been carried in the depression years and earlier.

All these thousands of people, with two things in common. They were trade unionists. And they knew the Government was out to make things harder for them.

It was estimated that 140,000 came to protest. But the head counting wasn't important. It was obviously the biggest demonstration of the century—the biggest since the Chartists moved working men to demand the right to vote, 130 years earlier.

And everybody who watched the endless column move slowly from Hyde Park to Trafalgar Square could see that these were

Excerpt from book entitled 'The Great March"

81

April 6, 1971

Mr. Neville Clarke
15 Denton Rd.
Stonebridge
London N.W. 10
England.

Dear Comrade Clarke,

          Thank you very much for your letter of March 25.
May I congratulate you on the fine effort that you are
making for the Party.

          I think your idea of the Raffle is excellent.
Unfortunately, I would not myself be able to come to
England at that time, but I have passed your letter on
to Comrade Patterson, to see what else we might be able
to arrange.

          Again, please accept my congratulations on your
fine work. Will you give my regards to all our friends and
supporters in England.

          Warm regards to you.

                                        Yours sincerely,

                                        Michael Manley
                                        LEADER OF THE OPPOSITION.

c.c. P.J. Patterson

President: Michael Manley, M.P., Vice-Presidents: Sen. P.J. Patterson, H.F. Cooke, M.P., F.A. Glasspole, M.P., D.J. Thompson, Q.C. Chairman: D.H. Coore, M.P., Gen. Secy: S.O. Veitch, Deputy Gen. Secy: K.A. Munn, M.P. Treasurer: E.G. Peart, M.P.

Letter from
Mr. Michael Manley (PNP, Ja)
CONCERNING FUND-RAISING RAFFLE IN THE UK

HOUSES OF PARLIAMENT

GORDON HOUSE,

DUKE STREET,

KINGSTON, JAMAICA

No._____

39½, Johns Lane,
Kingston,
May, 1971.

Mr. Neville Clarke,
15, Denton Road,
Stonebridge,
London N. W. 10,
England.

Dear Comrade Clarke,

The Party Leader, Comrade Michael Manley has handed me your letter to him and I would like to add my congratulations on the wonderful job you are attempting on behalf of the Party and wish to commend your idea of the raffle. We are badly in need of funds in order to fight the next elections.

You will appreciate that it would be imprudent for us to incurr tremendous expense in sending someone to represent us at the drawing of the raffle as that would have the effect of depriving us of money which you are seeking to collect. It seems therefore that the only course open is to enquire from Party colleagues whether anyone will be present in England round about the time of the raffle who could represent the Party. I propose to make immediate enquiries to this effect and will therefore let you know as soon as possible.

Please convey to your group my best wishes for continued success.

Yours faithfully,

P. J. PATTERSON.

PJP/gvp:

Letter from
Mr. P. J. Patterson (PNP, Ja)
CONCERNING FUND-RAISING RAFFLE IN THE UK

AD

Department of Employment and Productivity
LONDON AND SOUTH EASTERN REGIONAL OFFICE
Hanway House Red Lion Square London WCI R 4NH

Telephone 01-405 8454 ext 258

N Clarke Esq
Secretary
The Brent Trades Council
15 Denton Road
Stonebridge
LONDON NW10

Your reference

Our reference A 125/71

Date 12 October 1971

Dear Sir

It is proposed that the Willesden and Wembley Local
Employment Committee which was set up to advise and assist
the Secretary of State for Employment with the working of
Employment Exchanges should be prematurely terminated on
27 November, 1971. A new committee, to be known as the
"Brent and Harrow" Local Employment Committee, will then
be set up. In addition to the area of the old Willesden
and Wembley committee the new one will also cover the area
of the Harrow Employment Exchange. I enclose for your
information a leaflet (EDL 102) which gives a brief outline
of the constitution and functions of these committees.

It has been agreed with the Trades Union Congress that you
should be asked for nominations for membership of the
Workpeople's Panel of the committee from Trade Union
branches in your area, irrespective of whether they are
affiliated or not affiliated to your Trades Council. The
persons selected will, however, represent workers generally
in the districts, and not a particular industry, organisation
or other sectional interest. It is desirable, of course,
that we should be in a position to ensure that
representation is as broad as possible, and it would
therefore be helpful if you would kindly indicate the Trade
Union to which your nominees belong.

We shall probably need eight representatives for the
Willesden and Wembley district, but it is desired that
you should submit names in excess of this number from
which the Secretary of State can select the required
number for appointment. In this connection, I should
like to make it clear that the additional nominations
are required to enable a choice to be made on the basis
of such matters as the overall geographical and industrial
spread of representatives over the area covered by this
Committee, and the spread of representation between men
and women. To assist us in this aim it would be
appreciated if your nominations could include at least
three persons from T&GWU., two from AEF., one from
NSMM., one from AUBTW and one from ASLEF.

I would be glad to receive as soon as possible any
nominations you wish to make.

Yours faithfully

R M DORRELL (MISS)
for Regional Controller

ENC

Request for nominations:

DEPARTMENT OF EMPLOYMENT AND PRODUCTIVITY, UK

N.F. CLARKE

is the Secretary of the

BRENT

Trades Council

General Secretary of the Trades Union Congress

Signature of Secretary

Address: 15 Denton Road

Stonebridge, London N.W.10.

On retiring from the Secretaryship, the holder of this
credential should return it to the Trades Union Congress,
Congress House, Great Russell Street, London WC1

Official Secretarial Credential –

BRENT TRADES COUNCIL

THE BRENT TRADES COUNCIL
(Incorporating Willesden & Wembley Trades Councils)
375 HIGH ROAD, WILLESDEN, N.W.10

CHAIRMAN:
K.Spence Esq.

HONORARY SECRETARY:
N.F.Clarke,
15 Denton Road,
Stonebridge,
N.W.10.

The Chief Superintendent of Police,
Harlesden Police Station,.
  Craven Park
  N.W.10.
Dear Sir,
         The Brent Trades Council at it's June meeting was informed of the
arrest of members of this Council and other individuals,on Saturday the 23rd
June 1973,whilst collecting signitures against rising prices.
The Trades Council protests in the strongest possible terms to the hostile
and unnecessary way in which these people were reportly arrested and is
alarm to know that such a common practise has now become unlawful.
     I am instructed to inform you that this Trades Council is very perturb
over this action by your Constabulary and shall be asking the M.P.s and the
T.U.C. to raise the matter at a higher level.

                                 Yours Sincerely

                                 N.F.Clarke
                                    Secretary

Letter to Superintendent of Police
STATING CONCERNS ABOUT ARRESTS OF LAWFUL PROTESTORS

K. Sprice,
75, Station Road,
Hendon,
London N.W.4.

N.F. Clarke,
15, Denton Road,
Stonebridge,
London N.W.10.

Date as Postmark;

The General Secretary,
National Union of Mineworkers,
222, Euston Road,
London N.W.1 2BX.

Dear Sir & Brother,

         I am instructed to inform you that the members of the Brent Trades
Council have studied and discussed the publication "National Energy Policy"
issued by the National Union of Mineworkers with interest and sympathy, and
welcome and support it's approach to the necessity for strong energetic
action towards a co-ordinated fuel policy.

         We concur with the Mineworkers that every possibility should be
examined to see that coal is used more effectively and urge them to resist
further redundancies in the coal industry.

                      Yours Fatihfully,

                      N. F. Clarke.

Letter to the General Secretary
OF THE MINEWORKERS TRADE UNION

**LABOUR
PARTY
1974**

MEMBERSHIP CARD

NAME *MR NF CLARKE*

ADDRESS *15 DEWTON RD*

LONDON NW10

PARTY *B·S·C·LP*

ARE YOU READING ?

'abour Weekly'

The Party's newspaper

5p every Friday from
your newsagent

MEMBERSHIP SUBSCRIPTIONS

DATE	AMOUNT	RECEIVED BY
6/3/74	£1·20	

To secure for the workers by hand or by brain the full fruits
of their industry and the most equitable distribution thereof,
that may be possible, upon the basis of the common owner-
ship of the means of production, distribution and exchange,
and the best obtainable system of popular administration and
control of each industry or service.

THE CONSTITUTION OF THE LABOUR PARTY
CLAUSE IV No. 4

*Labour Party (UK)
Membership Card*

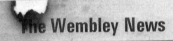

The Wembley News　　　　　　　　　　　King and Hutchings

Wembley Hill House Neeld Parade Wembley　　Wembley News
Telephone 01-902 6051 *three lines*　　　　　　Kingsbury News

LWB/Ed.　　　　　　　　　　　　　　　March 4, 1974.

Mr. N.F. Clarke,
15, Denton Road,
Stonebridge,
London, N.W.10.

Dear Mr. Clarke,

    Thank you for your letter of last week. I cannot quite understand the tone of the letter or the reasons for your committee's complaint. I was not aware that there had been any deterioration in the relationship between our two organisations. I had noticed a lack of news from you but had assumed that you were no longer inviting us either because you wished to hold private discussions or because no meetings were, in fact, being held.

    On two occasions recently we have attended and reported on your Trades Council's meetings. I can recall that we were unable to cover a Sunday conference, but was not unduly perturbed because we had already reported your views on the subject under discussion. I thought that you were aware that we are always happy to receive from you news items which you feel merit publicity although, of course, we cannot guarantee always to have the space to publish every item submitted by any organisation.

    After explaining my wish that good relations should continue between us it is now, with much regret, that I have to apologise for thefact that we were unable to cover your annual general meeting last week. I am asking a reporter to get in touch with you and hope that we shall be able to elicit sufficient information to enable us to give you the publicity you seek.

                          Yours sincerely,

                          (L.W. BLAND),
                          Editor.

A Division of Westminster Press Ltd.
Company No. 331496 Registered in England *Registered Office* 8-16 Great New Street London EC4P 4ER

Apology letter from The Wembley News

ED 551

DEPARTMENT OF EMPLOYMENT

EMPLOYMENT EXCHANGE   Harlesden House
                            High Street
Telephone 01-965-6506   Harlesden NW10 4TL
        Ext 102

N F Clarke Esq.
Honorary Secretary   Your reference
The Brent Trades Council
15 Denton Road   Our reference DMO/G2/F2/MH
Stonebridge
London NW10   Date 5 March 1974

Dear Mr Clarke

In Mr Eaton's absence on leave this week, I am writing to thank you for your letter nominating Mr H I Timothy for a seat on the new District Disablement Advisory Committee. I have passed your letter on to our Regional Office, who will complete the formalities involved. We look forward to seeing Mr Timothy at the inaugural meeting in April.

I have discussed the question of the L E C nominations with our Regional Office and they agree that this could well be held back until we know more about the Manpower Services Commission's proposals for advisory committees. I believe we will know more by the time the L E C meets again in May.

Yours sincerely

Michael Horne.

M St J Horner

Thank You letter from the
DEPARTMENT OF EMPLOYMENT

In passing I must be critical of the Royal College of Nursing since the last time they were active on this issue it happened to be when Dick Crossman was the Secretary of State. During the last three and a half years I have been making speeches in the House and urging opposition to the various stages of the Conservatives' economic policies which held down the pay claims of all lower paid workers including nurses. During the whole of that time the Royal College has remained mute. It seems significant that it is only when a Labour Government takes office that the Royal College's representatives decide to become militant against the efforts of the Labour Government to solve their difficulties.

There are a number of anomalies at the present time, and as an example I refer to the deplorable decision to increase the charges for meals in spite of the fact that the pay award due on April 1st has still not come into effect. I fully support the action taken by the Central Middlesex Hospital nurses when they refused to use the canteen.

Might I suggest that you invite a representative of N.U.P.E. to the meeting in addition to C.O.H.S.E.

Yours sincerely,

Neville Clarke, Esq.,
Brent Trades Council.
15. Denton Road.
N.W.10.

Letter from Laurie Pavitt, MP, UK
DEPLORING ROYAL COLLEGE OF NURSING

HOUSE OF COMMONS
LONDON SWIA OAA

30th April, 1974.

Dear Secretary,

Thank you for the invitation to the May Day Social on Thursday. I wish the event every success, but I shall be engaged in Parliament with two House of Commons 'three line' whips and this will prevent my attending.

I trust that your members will be out supporting the Labour candidates on Thursday and that the Labour G.L.C. will continue to give support to the tremendous task that the new Labour Government has undertaken for the benefit of the people of London generally.

Yours sincerely,

Laurie Pavitt

The Secretary,
Brent Trades Council.
Brent Trades and Labour Hall.
375, High Road.
N.W.10.

Letter from Laurie Pavitt, MP, UK

OUTLINING REASON FOR HIS INTENDED ABSENCE FROM MAY DAY SPECIAL

HOUSE OF COMMONS
LONDON SW1A OAA

7th May 1974

Mr N. Clarke
Secretary
Brent Trades Council

Dear Bro. Clarke

Many thanks indeed for your
letter, and for the support
of your Council for our
efforts in respect of the
Shrewsbury lads.

Because of a deluge of
correspondence I can only
send you this brief reply, but
please be assured we shall
continue to do all we possibly
can

With best wishes

Norman Atkinson

HOUSE OF COMMONS
LONDON SW1A OAA

3 May 1974

Dear Mr. Clarke,

Thank you for your letter. I am
sorry I was not able to be present at
the House of Commons at lunch time on
May 1 to see members of the Brent Trades
Council and trade unionists. I was at
that time at work in my office in the
Department of the Environment a little
distance away. However, please convey
my May Day greetings to local trade
unionists. They will be pleased to have
heard today's announcement that the
Second Reading of the Labour Government's
Bill to repeal the Tory Industrial
Relations Act will take place next week.

Yours sincerely,

E. Stracha

 pp Reg Freeson MP

N.F. Clarke Esq.,
15 Denton Road,
Stonebridge,
LONDON N.W.10.

Correspondence from House of Commons

From L.A. PAVITT, M.P.

30th May, 1974.

Dear Neville, Clarke,

Thank you for your letter and the invitation
to attend the meeting at Acton Lane School on June 18th.
I will certainly do my best to be present, but because the
House will be sitting at that time, I will accede to your
second suggestion of giving my views on the present
situation.

Firstly you will know that for many issues I
have led in this issue and have put pressure on previous
Governments to increase nurses pay, and you will also know
that as my own daughter is a nurse, I need no further pressure
or first-hand information. Immediately following the Election,
and before the new Parliament assembled, I was able to have a
personal interview with Barbara Castle the Secretary of State,
and I discussed the matter very fully since I am the Chairman of
the Parliamentary Labour Party's Health Group. In spite of
the present acute economic situation, priority is being given
to nurses pay, pay for the professions supplementary to medicine
(physiotherapists, speech therapists, radiographers etc.) and
the other ancillary workers, and these will take precedence over
the other important aspects such as hospital building and other
capital expenditure. Already the nurses request for a review has been
met, and I enclose a copy of Hansard giving a report of the Debate
in the House and of Barbara Castle's statement.

I have arranged for the representative of the
Nurses Whitley Council Bill Griffiths N.U.P.E and the C.O.H.S.E
representative Alfred Spanswick and the Royal College of Nursing
representative to attend a meeting at the House to discuss problems
with Members of Parliament when the House re-assembles, but I have
now been asked to defer this meeting in order to await the
immediate outcome of the review body.

Because I feel industrial action cannot be effective
without putting patients at risk I believe the action taken by
C.O.H.S.E is not in the best interests of either the nurses or
the National Health Service. You will know that I am a member of
N.U.P.E, and I strongly support the N.U.P.E. attitude on the
present situation.

Letter from Laurie Pavitt, MP, UK

REGARDING NURSES INDUSTRIAL ACTION

Chairman: Roger Cox

Secretary: Neville Clark
15 Denton Road
London NW10

I M P O R T A N T   N O T I C E
* * * * * * * * * * * * * * *

THE TRADES COUNCIL AND THE HOOVER STRIKE

At the last meeting of the Executive of the Trades Council, held on Wednesday, 13 November 1974, it was unanimously agreed to give full support to the 2,000 workers who are at present locked out by the Management at the Hoover Factory on the Western Avenue at Perivale.

The dispute began 3 weeks ago when 150 tool room workers, members of the AUEW, refused to accept an offer from Management, claiming that Management had gone back on promises made during the wage freeze. They went on strike and the other workers, mainly members of the GMWU and TGWU, were locked out. 5 of the women workers from the GMWU addressed a Conference on Womens Equal Rights, jointly sponsored by the Trades Council, the Brent Federation of Tenants and Residents Associations and the Brent Womens Centre on Sunday November 10. A very strong feature of the strike is the demand for equal pay and opportunity by the Unions inside of the factory.

The Unions and the workers are concerned that the Management is trying to break the very strong Union organisation inside of the factory and make redundant a number of workers. They expect to be out until the New Year.

The Southall District of the AEU has declared the strike official but the AEU workers, pending a decision by the National Executive are not yet receiving strike pay. Further because the other workers have been locked out, they are also not receiving strike pay. The workers are in desparate need of financial assistance and we therefore urge you to give them every support. Delegations of the Shop Stewards will be visiting the factories in Brent over the next two weeks to meet with and speak to Branch, Shop Steward or lunchtime or canteen meetings. Further, if you wish to make a donation, please forward it to the Trades Council and we will pass it on to the Strike Committee.

If you wish to send fraternal delegates to the picket lines, the pickets, who are trying to prevent parts leaving the factory, start daily at 7.30am at the factories on the junction of the Western Avenue and Bedford Lane (nearest tubes are Hanger Lane and Perivale, on the Central Line and the 105 bus stops opposite the factory.) However, it should be made clear that the picketing is extremely well organised already and that their main need is money.

Finally, if you require any further information, contact either:-
Bro. Alan Pledge, Senior Steward, GMWU, Hoovers   578 4581
OR
Bro Jack Dromey, Vice Chairman of Brent Trades Council 451 1122 work
                                                       739 7599 home

Brent Trades Councils notice
to Hoover Management

REGARDING THEIR SUPPORT OF THE EMPLOYEE INDUSTRIAL ACTION

6th September 1974

Mr. Clarke,
C/O Mr. Leighton Holness.

Dear Brother Clarke,

I wish to advise that the National Workers Union is desirous of making you a job offer on the six months trial basis that we discussed when I saw you in London earlier this year.

We feel that the experience that you have gained in the British Trade Union Movement could be of value to us, and we know of the fine work you have been doing on behalf of the P.N.P. in London, also you have been highly recommended to us by Mr. Sidney Fagan who is aware of the work you are doing in trying to get the B.B.Coke Memorial established.

I will shortly be writing you setting out details and possible areas of your assignment.

We would hope that it would be possible for you to join us early in 1975.

Yours sincerely,
NATIONAL WORKERS UNION

SENATOR CARLYLE DUNKLEY
ISLAND SUPERVISOR

CD:HG

Job Offer Letter:

NATIONAL WORKERS UNION (JAMAICA)

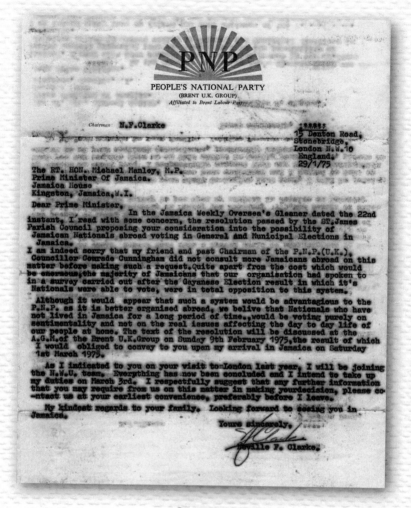

PNP

PEOPLE'S NATIONAL PARTY
(BRENT U.K. GROUP)
Affiliated to Brent Labour Party

Chairman N.F.Clarke

15 Denton Road,
Stonebridge,
London N.W.10
England.
29/1/75

The RT. HON. Michael Manley, M.P.
Prime Minister Of Jamaica.
Jamaica House
Kingston, Jamaica, W.I.

Dear Prime Minister,

In the Jamaica Weekly Oversea's Gleaner dated the 22nd instant, I read with some concern, the resolution passed by the ST.James Parish Council proposing your consideration into the possibility of Jamaican Nationals abroad voting in General and Municipal Elections in Jamaica.

I am indeed sorry that my friend and past Chairman of the P.N.P.(U.K.), Councillor Comrade Cunningham did not consult more Jamaicans abroad on this matter before making such a request. Quite apart from the cost which would be enormous, the majority of Jamaicans that our organisation had spoken to in a survey carried out after the Gayanese Election result in which it's Nationals were able to vote, were in total opposition to this system.

Although it would appear that such a system would be advantagious to the P.N.P. as it is better organised abroad, we belive that Nationals who have not lived in Jamaica for a long period of time, would be voting purely on sentimentality and not on the real issues affecting the day to day life of our people at home. The text of the resolution will be discussed at the A.G.M.of the Brent U.K.Group on Sunday 9th February 1975,the result of which I would obliged to convey to you upon my arrival in Jamaica on Saturday 1st March 1975.

As I indicated to you on your visit to London last year, I will be joining the N.W.U. team. Everything has now been concluded and I intend to take up my duties on March 3rd. I respectfully suggest that any further information that you may require from us on this matter in making yourdecision, please co-ntact us at your earliest convenience, preferably before I leave.

My kindest regards to your family. Looking forward to seeing you in Jamaica.

Yours sincerely,

Neville F. Clarke.

Letter to
Mr. Michael Manley, (P.M, Ja)
OUTLINING WHY IT WAS NOT A GOOD IDEA FOR NON-RESIDENTS TO VOTE IN LOCAL ELECTIONS

District Manager's
Office
BRENT/HARROW DISTRIC
161 HIGH STREET
LONDON
NW10 4TL Tel: 965 6500

DISTRICT MANAGER: G W

24 FEBRUARY 1975

NEVILLE CLARKE ESQ
15 DENTON ROAD
LONDON
N W 10

Dear Neville,

I write to wish you well in your new venture
in Jamacia and I trust sucess and satisfaction
reward your endeavours.

As you are now leaving us, I feel I cannot let
you go without placing on record my appreciation
of the useful contact that developed between us.
Ray Harrison and Ken George both join me in
expressing thanks and wishing you well.

Yours sincerely,

George Eaton

Farewell & Appreciation Letter

FROM EMPLOYMENT SERVICE AGENCY, UK

JAMAICA HOUSE
KINGSTON, JAMAICA

13th February, 1975

Dear Neville,

Thank you very much for your letter of
January 29. I have noted your concern about the
question of Jamaican nationals abroad voting in
local elections and should let you know that this is
not possible under the Constitution.

With kind regards,

Yours sincerely,

Michael Manley

Neville F. Clarke, Esq.,
15 Denton Road,
Stonebridge,
London N.W.10,
England

Letter from

Mr. Michael Manley (P.M. Ja)

REGARDING JAMAICANS ABROAD VOTING IN JAMAICAN ELECTIONS

Alderman Phillip Hartley

AT SEND OFF PARTY 1975

COMETH THE MAN

On the morning of September 20th, members of the Progressive League started gathering as early as 8 am at Gascart Road in Clapham Common for the arrival of Mr. Manley. This meeting was scheduled for 10 am. Expectations were high and everyone was excited at meeting this son of Norman Washington Manley, perhaps most of them for the first time. On his arrival, he was accompanied by a young P.J. Patterson and Robert Saunds, an MP from Clarendon. On entering the room, in a booming voice he greeted the gathering, "Good morning comrades." The response was spontaneous and then he asked, "Who is Neville Clarke?" I immediately raised my hand and he beckoned to me and asked the comrades to excuse us and proceeded to lead me outside. He expressed his pleasure at meeting me at last and then indicated that he was not in favour of having a Progressive League in England. He said that was for the United States of America. He would prefer a People's National Party organization in the UK and in that regard he intended to advise the comrades of his decision. He further stated that I would be appointed as national organizer for the party in England. I was flabbergasted, as I supposed everyone else in the room would be when they heard. I did not know whether to refuse or to accept, but I wanted to see what other members' reaction would be to the news.

The chairman of the league gave his welcoming address, after which Mr. Manley dropped the bombshell, which in my view was a fait accompli.

Needless to say, everyone agreed, except Aston Hall, the chairman, whose idea it was to establish the league in London.

The reception at Regents Park that evening was well attended and to my great delight, many of the persons who were invited, were present. I was particularly delighted that the mayor of Brent, Mrs. Ruby Taylor and her husband, both of the Conservative Party, who had not long before taken control of the Brent borough had accepted my invitation. My delight in her attendance was amplified later that evening when Mayor Taylor came to my rescue. After the reception had ended, I realized that Messrs. Manley and Patterson had departed for the meeting with Jamaican nationals at the Anson Hall in Cricklewood without me, who was supposed to be the chairman of that meeting. I had no transportation except the bus to get there.

Fortunately for me, Mayor Taylor had not yet departed the scene and having heard of my dilemma, offered to take me to the venue; an offer which I gladly accepted. But I could not have imagined that I would have travelled to that event in a stately Rolls Royce. On entering the car, I positioned myself by the window hoping that any black person, or white for that matter, would be able to get a glimpse of me along the way, but unfortunately that was not the case. On arrival at the hall, Jamaicans who were waiting outside rushed to the car in excitement, believing that Mr. Manley was the occupant, only to see the chauffeur with cap in hand, open the door for my exit at which someone remarked, "It's only Neville. Den is what you doin' inna Rolls Royce, boy you big."

Shortly after that exciting moment, Messrs. Manley and Patterson arrived in a Rover 2000 and were greeted with tremendous applause. The hall was packed with Jamaicans and other nationals to meet the son of the great Norman Washington Manley. The senior Manley was an enigma to many Jamaicans who had migrated to England since the 50's and early 60's. This, however, only added to the difficulty and the mystery of the event. Undoubtedly, the meeting was a great success with persons leaving with a renewed interest in, and excitement about the country of their birth and the People's National Party.

On Monday, September 22, I arrived at my workplace very early in anticipation of Mr. Manley's arrival, which was scheduled for 10 am As expected, the Jamaican workers were bursting with pride and excitement to see a leader of their homeland also. The trade union officials, led by Bill Morton gathered at the main entrance to the head office at 9:50 am to meet the fellow trade unionist from the West Indies, but at 10 am there was no sign of the guests.

By this time, Mr. Morton was pacing back and forth, with me behind him. Every car that came our direction found us hoping that Mr. Manley was onboard. This continued until 10:50 am, when he finally arrived, accompanied by Mr. Patterson, who alighted from the car ahead of Mr. Manley and waited a while, then both men proceeded towards the welcoming party.

With arms outstretched, Mr. Morton advanced towards Mr. Patterson, the much darker skinned of the two coming from Jamaica and said "Mr. Manley?" to which Mr. Patterson replied, "No sir, this is Mr. Manley," pointing towards Michael. Bill Morton then turned to Mr. Manley and shook his hands, while saying "Mr. Manley, I see you have arrived on Jamaica's time." To this, Mr. Manley responded, "I'm sorry, but we took the wrong turn to get here."

With greetings and comradeship established, the convenor and I escorted both gentlemen to the chairman's office, only to find that the board meeting had started. Having not seen the visitor arrive at 10 am as scheduled, they decided to start the meeting. On realizing the awkward situation all around, I asked the chairman's secretary to pop into the boardroom to ask him if he could spare a moment to meet Mr. Manley. This she did, and after a short while, the chairman emerged looking somewhat disappointed. He shook both gentlemen's hands and remarked that he intended to take them around the plant, but was now in the middle of the meeting and so will now delegate that task to Neville.

I observed the surprised look on the faces of both our guests on hearing that a young, black man had the confidence of the chairman of this large organization. Being entrusted with this kind of responsibility was an honour and a privilege to be cherished and I enjoyed every moment of it.

The factory tour went very well, especially for the Jamaicans and other non-whites who were eager to shake hands and speak with Mr. Manley as he went through the various departments. I felt very proud of the events which unfolded. At the end of the tour, Mr. Manley remarked that he was very pleased that he had an opportunity to engage and encourage the skilled Jamaican workers to consider returning home and offering their acquired skills to the country of their birth. Similarly, he impressed upon me to return home to help to build the National Workers Union, the organization to which he belonged.

The rest of the day was spent meeting with the Association of Jamaicans, which was headed by a lady by the name of Vi Mendez, then after that, another meeting with the West Indian Standing Conference members. In my view, the visit to England, though short, was a successful and enlightening one.

With the visit now over, my thoughts were now focused on my appointment as national organizer for the party in England. I questioned myself, "How does one go about convincing Jamaicans living 5000 miles away to become members of a political organization from which they will derive no immediate benefit?" They would not even be able to vote, that was a major concern. Bearing this in mind, I consulted with members of the now defunct Progressive League by telephone and solicited their views on the way forward. After this conversation, we agreed to meet on the second Sunday of October 1969 at Tooting Beck, London at 3 pm for discussions.

There was a very good turnout for the event. Some of the attendees had not been involved in the league before, but were members of various party groups back in Jamaica, in what was then 'the old days.'

In attendance were senior comrades like Jimmy Byfield, formerly of Group 69 of Sutton Street, Jamaica, Eric McAlpine, Cecil Collington, Headly Cunningham, to name a few. With the momentum very high, I wasted no time in outlining the purpose of the meeting and holding elections for persons to occupy positions in the group. Comrade Headly Cunningham was elected the first chairman of what was named the Tooting group of PNP, UK. Eric McAlpine was elected the public relations officer.

My next assignment was the formation of a group in my area of residence in Brent. The Brent PNP group meeting was held on the last Sunday of October and the venue was the Trades Council's hall in Willesden, London, North West. The elected officers were Comrade Navel Clarke, chairman; Aubrey Brown, secretary and comrades Winchester 'Jimmy' James, Charley Graham otherwise known as Quaker, originally from the parish of Clarendon, Nat Jackson and Comrade Bent among others.

By the first Sunday in December, I organized the Hackney group in the constituency of Labour Party's candidate, Dr. David Pitt. While hopeful, I strongly doubted it would ever happen, but the Jamaicans, mostly men, were so excited and full of sentiments about the country of their birth, that they wanted to be identified with it in this particular way.

In all the groups, our first order of business was to embark on a fundraising exercise for the party. We decided on raffles, dances and excursions, which were well supported by members and friends.

We were now in the New Year 1970, and my engagements had become so frequent and intensive that my family could hardly enjoy the togetherness that we were accustomed. On one occasion, I had a conversation about it with my good friend, John Butta, of the Brent Teachers' Association and also a member of the Trades Council. I expressed my concern about my involvement in all these activities and its impact on my family life. He encouraged me to take time to consider the purpose of my involvement in the activities, most of which were voluntary, with no remuneration attached.

It was at this point that I sat calmly and reflected on how I got to this place and whether I should continue to be involved in the process. To this end, I decided to consult with another good friend and colleague, Ken Spence, chairman of the Trades Council. He listened attentively then responded in the most dramatic way one could imagine saying, "Don't be bloody stupid, you have reached a position that most white persons would give their right arm to get. We are confident that you have the ability to do the job of leading the organization, so get rid of this negative idea. Some things are not measured in monetary terms!" This one comment was enough to convince me that this was the fulfilment of my motto. Beyond that, it was a demonstration of a black man's ability to rise to the seat of power in the land and my role was the laying of the foundation upon which others of my colour could build on.

This advice and mind shift took place at a good time as the Trade Union Congress, TUC had even more plans for me. I was selected to attend Ruskin College, Oxford for a secretarial course, which was also extended to include general industrial relations and its laws. I was assured that all expenses would be met, and I would continue to receive the equivalent of my salary during the period, which I gladly agreed to.

During my tenure at Oxford, I received news that Glacier, the company for which I had worked for the past nine and half years, would be taking advantage of the government's five year tax-free concession by moving its operations to Bradford. This had several implications for me personally as well as the trade union operation there. First, personally it meant that by the end of 1970, I would have no job, unless I agreed to move to Bradford with them. But the option did not appeal to me, so I later opted for redundancy. Second, the Transport and Workers General Union Branch, of which I was a member and their representative to the Trades Council, would be dissolved. That further meant that in order for me to continue as secretary, I had to transfer my union membership to the United Dairies Branch in Cricklewood, where Ken Spence was chief union officer.

I made sure my fees were fully paid and everything else was in full compliance with the union rules as secretary of the Trades Council, especially during this period.

Being out of a paying job, I had plenty of time to concentrate on both the affairs of the union and the PNP UK groups. As such, I had enough opportunity to make the necessary preparations for the Great March dubbed 'Kill the Bill' that was being jointly planned by various trades unions.

Sunday, February 21, 1971 was a remarkable day in British history. People came out in the tens of thousands to protest. I gathered my troop of workers, armed with banner and leaflets and journeyed to Charing Cross Station where all Trades Councils were instructed to meet, and from there, we walked along Oxford Street to Speakers Corner in Hyde Park to join the main column of protestors moving on to Trafalgar Square. It was a very cold day, but I was determined to be part of an event which would go down in the annals of history. It was already being dubbed the biggest demonstration of the century as people came from all parts of Britain, moving columns 7 miles long and 10 - 15 abreast. I carried my banner representing the Brent Trades Council with pride as a black man in the struggle for justice for the working class. We were not about to strengthen the powers of the employers and weaken the hands of the trade unions, we were determined to 'Kill the Bill.' This was the great march and I am proud to have been a part of it.

On Sunday, February 28, 1971 the Tooting group of the People's National Party held its meeting, which I attended in my capacity as national organizer, and was very surprised to see the large gathering of Jamaicans who had come to participate as members of the party. The greater portion of the meeting was spent listening to their experiences in the party back in Jamaica, ending with my delight in the unanimous decision for a serious fundraising exercise in preparation for the next general election in Jamaica, which was scheduled for 1972.

A number of questions arose, but the most frequently asked was: What benefit would be derived from being a member of a party 5000 miles away? Another equally important was, "would we be able to vote?" I immediately found myself in a bind for not having a reassuring answer to the questions, but made the commitment to raise the matter with the Brent and Hackney groups and then inform the party at home of their views. I was fully aware that Guyana had allowed their nationals living in England to have the right to vote in their country's elections, so the question was not surprising at the time.

However, after three lengthy discussions with all group members, it was decided that Jamaicans living in England were not fully aware of the issues relating to the political life back home and would therefore be voting purely out of sentiment. This was deemed unacceptable to the process and accordingly the notion of a vote by Jamaicans living in England, and anywhere abroad for that matter, was rejected.

With that now settled, the question as to what benefit we would therefore derive being a member of the party living in England became etched in our minds for weeks, especially during the fundraising campaign. With the knowledge that the party was affiliated to Socialist International, which also included the British Labour Party, of which I was now a powerful and respected member, I took the liberty of approaching the Labour Party's hierarchy with the idea of affiliating the local PNP groups to the Constituency's Labour Party in which they existed.

To gain acceptance of both bodies, I convinced them that 99.9 percent of black people who voted, gave support to the Labour Party, therefore this affiliation would strengthen their support for the future, thus giving the PNP members a sense of belonging in England. The proposition, I will report, was unanimously accepted, including our party in Jamaica. Subsequently, I was fortunate to obtain a copy of the annual worldwide report of the Bank of Nova Scotia for 1970/71, which provided a comprehensive description of the state of affairs in Jamaica from banking, agriculture, industry and commerce to climatic conditions. This I used as my main source of information coming from Jamaica at our group meetings.

I developed a strategy of segmenting the various items and commented comprehensively on one each month, thereby creating the impression that I was receiving information directly from Jamaica through the party.

I also used information from the Jamaica Gleaner's weekly edition, which was published in London at the time. This provided for healthy and robust debates concerning Jamaica at all PNP group meetings, which helped to maintain a deep interest in Jamaica and the People's National Party.

The close relationship between the People's National Party Tooting group and the local Labour Party, resulted in the election of Comrade Ken Enwright, the first black councillor to the Wondsworth Borough Council. Ken hailed from Manchester in Jamaica. Later, after the official affiliation, two members of the Brent PNP groups, comrades Charlie Graham and Nat Jackson were selected as candidates for the Labour Party, which also resulted in Comrade Nat Jackson being elected as councillor for the Monks

Park division. Unfortunately, Comrade Graham, despite a very good show, was not successful.

Apparently, my active participation in politics in the borough of Brent and London, generally, had inspired a few black men. More were getting involved in the affairs of the country and their community that impacted their lives, and for that I felt very proud.

As the year 1971 drew to a close, the group reported a healthy financial status. This made me very happy as it meant we could participate actively in the early 1972 general elections in Jamaica. Our comrade, Cecil Collier, was chosen to represent the UK groups on the campaign trail in Jamaica and through the general election. At the end of December 1971, he took leave from his job and headed to Jamaica, carrying a substantial amount of money for the party.

We also urged our members to write to their relatives and friends in Jamaica to vote for the People's National Party in the elections. The election, held on February 29, 1972, was a great success for the party and my friend Michael Manley. We in England celebrated the victory for almost a whole month.

It was also my good fortune to secure a new job in early 1972. This time, it was at a small establishment known as Lessme Ltd., a chocolate factory located at Scrubs Lane, just off the Harrow Road, but in the borough of Kensington. The company employed approximately 50 persons, mostly West Indians from the smaller islands. Unfortunately, none were interested in joining a union as they were scared.

My role was a supervisory one. I was replacing a Polish man by the name of Pyslack who was retiring. Pyslack was in charge of the department that supplied fats and oils, two of the main ingredients for chocolate production. On getting the job, no mention was made of my being a trade union official or my involvement in politics. I decided to play it very low-key indeed.

Within two months' of Pyslack's retirement, I took full control of the department. Oil spilling had been reduced and orders for fats and cocoa butter were better regulated. The factory manager commended me on every occasion he passed through the department for the significant savings achieved in my first three months. This encouraged me to seek an increase in pay after the probation period.

Little did I know that during this time someone had found out about my connections with the trade union and brought it the attention of Mr. Anderson, the owner and CEO, from whom I had to get the increase. My request was conveyed through the factory manager, who of course was white, and he arranged the meeting with Mr. Anderson.

I was very confident that my performance to date would secure me a very good increase, so on the appointed day, I walked into Mr. Anderson's office for the first time and with great expectations made my request, only to be given the response, "If you don't like the job or feel it is too much for you, you can hand in your notice and we will accept it." I was shocked out of my wits to hear those words coming from the CEO, who at least once per week would walk through all the departments observing and not saying a word to any of the employees. Any negative comments would be made by and through the factory manager and I had received none.

On hearing these words, I became upset and not caring if I got fired, I said, "I'm surprised to hear that response coming from a respectable gentleman like you. It is the duty of any employee to approach his employer concerning the condition of employment, including salary increases. If you are of the view that I am not doing a good job, then you can fire me. I will await your decision." With that said, I asked to be excused and left the office.

Two days later, the factory manager came to my department and informed me that no one had ever spoken to Mr. Anderson the way I did and he was very surprised. I was, however, awarded an increase to match the level of the outgoing supervisor. The news of my encounter with the CEO quickly spread and suddenly I became a hero among my fellow workers.

The following week, the factory manager informed all staff to prepare the factory for a visit by the mayor of the borough of Kensington, in which we were located. On the occasion, Mr. Anderson escorted the mayor and his party through the departments, explaining the different functions at each level. On their arrival to my department, the mayor, having recognized me, came to me saying "Nev, I didn't know that this is where you worked." I told him, "Oh yes! Very recently." We chatted for a while, with Mr. Anderson standing by watching in amazement at the camaraderie I had with His Worship, The Mayor…

The mayor was formally the secretary of the Kensington Trades Council, and he often collaborated with me on issues during his tenure. The very next day, Mr. Anderson came to the department and enquired, "How are things going Clarke?" I said "Very well Sir. Thanks for my increase." "Ok," he replied, "keep up the good work."

It was said that this was the first time he had ever casually addressed any of the black workers. From then on, the relationship was cordial. I was given time off whenever I wanted to carry out my other activities, as long as provisions were made for the smooth and efficient running of the department. On the occasion of my leaving the job in February 1975 to return to Jamaica, Mr. Anderson shook my hand and wished me great success. He also made a commitment to assist my family if they were in need of anything.

The People's National Party's victory at the polls in Jamaica earlier that year had propelled me to even greater recognition by the party as its senior representative in England. Arrangements were made for me to meet with officers, ministers of government and other members of the party, if and when they visited England. Further, it was my understanding that since Jamaica retained the Westminster Parliamentary system of government, it was customary to send new members of parliament from Jamaica, normally from both sides to be exposed to the House of Commons procedure. Consequently, I was informed of the early arrival of two young men who were newly elected and chosen for the occasion.

They were Dallas Young of the People's National Party and Orette Bruce Golding of the Jamaica Labour Party. I quickly made contact at their hotel and took them for a drink and further made arrangements for them to meet and address fellow Jamaicans the following Sunday. This meeting took place at the Apollo Club Hall in Willesden, Brent, London.

It was the second time that many Jamaicans living in England would have an opportunity to meet and ask questions of Jamaican parliamentarians about Jamaica's issues. Similar to the first time with Mr. Manley, I also made arrangements for members of the PNP groups across London to be in full attendance. I was very pleased with the turnout on the day in question.

As chairman of the meeting, I gave a warm welcome to our honoured guests. I invited the People's National Party member to speak first. Unfortunately, the presentation and delivery turned out to be most unimpressive. Then Mr. Golding was called to the podium. He delivered a report to the audience on a wide range of subjects and events taking place, or had taken place in Jamaica in recent times. At the end of his delivery, he was given a standing ovation and was hailed in very loud echo by the group as "Comrade Golding" because of the near-socialist ideas he presented.

When we returned to their hotel, I whispered to Mr. Golding to make a U-turn when he got into the lobby and come back to the car so that I could take him out, leaving Dallas, the PNP member behind. I had never before set eyes on either gentlemen, but my 'spirit', as it is often colloquially said, took to Bruce Golding.

We visited three clubs in London that night, including the Apollo Club, where he met with Jeffery Palmer, the owner, who hailed from Clarendon. It was about 3 am the next morning when we parted company. Having established a very good companionship, I arranged to meet and repeat the whole exercise the next night. I am happy to say that this encounter created a lasting friendship between Bruce Golding and myself.

Later on in 1972, I had the honour to host the Honourable Sydney Pagon, Minister of Regional Affairs and the Honourable Ernest Peart, Minister of Labour, both of whom, I understood were close friends of my father, Levan Clarke, who resided in the North East Constituency, in St. Elizabeth, Santa Cruz to be exact. I also hosted the first two prize-winning cane-cutters from Jamaica. They had won the trip to England to visit and meet with Jamaicans there as their reward for hard and dedicated work. They were chaperoned by a Mr. Manley Lumsden.

The appointment of Dr. Arthur Wint as Jamaica's high commissioner to England, was met with joy and excitement by Jamaican nationals in England, including me. I was rather pleased to receive a call from his office to meet with him shortly after his arrival in London as I'd heard that he wanted to meet with prominent Jamaicans in the various cities in England, starting with London.

Our meeting was cordial and informative. Each attendee was asked to describe his activities in his respective area and not surprisingly, most represented black community groups in London. My role as a trade unionist and senior member of the British Labour Party in the borough of Brent was very surprising to many, who apart from voting in local and general elections and paying union dues, were not involved. They were therefore meeting, for the first time, a black man who became a secretary of a trade union organization in England. We used the occasion to exchange contact numbers and thereafter, whenever they had a need for assistance and advice in their respective communities in matters of politics and labour, I would be called upon.

The meeting with Dr. Wint blossomed into a lasting friendship, as we continued to dialogue on a regular basis on matters affecting communities and in some respect, Jamaica, until I left England in 1975.

In 1973, the Trades Councils throughout England were once again called upon to mobilize their local union branches, for a nationwide one-day strike to be held on the 1st of May that year. This call was made by Victor Feather, leader of the Trade Union Congress, The strike was against the government's pay restraint policy and the rapid increases in the price of commodities.

My Trades Council was very active in the mobilization process, which resulted in a reported 1.6 million workers taking part in the action across the country. So great was the pressure that the Edward Heath government lost the elections of 1974 to the Labour Party, led by Harold Wilson. Upon taking over parliament, they proposed a reversal of the policy by the Conservatives to that of a voluntary limited pay increase. To that, the unions agreed.

Shortly after the strike, I read an article in the Jamaica *Weekly Gleaner*, which was a compilation of the daily publication in Jamaica, stating that the general secretary of the Trade Union Congress in Jamaica, a Mr. Hopeton Caven, would be visiting London on a particular date. Mr. Caven wanted to recruit Jamaicans in England who had trade union experience for his union back home in Jamaica. It went on to give the Dorchester Hotel in Marble Arch, London, as his place of abode while in England.

I was curious to know more about this union and what it had to offer, so on the appointed day, I made contact with Mr. Caven and was immediately invited to his hotel suite the following day. I was warmly welcomed with a drink of good 'ole Jamaica rum on arrival, and we exchanged pleasantries for a while. I was then asked to outline my experience and positions held to date. Unfortunately, after my presentation, Mr. Caven stated that he could not afford me. Further, he wanted someone who would start at the lower end of the organization, and I held too senior a position.

Ironically, the decision prompted a greater curiosity as to what it would be like to work with a union in Jamaica, especially the National Workers Union that I had heard so much about from Leighton Holness, Michael Manley and Syndey Pagon.

Some weeks later, I took the bold decision that it was time for me to visit Jamaica. I used the various meetings with the PNP groups as the source to inform our members of my intended visit to Jamaica. It was proposed that it would be best served if I schedule my trip for September that year, at which time I could represent the UK PNP groups for the first time as a party delegate to the conference.

One could not imagine the joy I felt when everyone agreed. The very thought of attending a political conference in Jamaica brought excitement and joy. The joy was mingled with a little fear however, after all, I had left Jamaica as an eighteen-year-old, unheard-of. I would now return as a representative of so many of my countrymen and women living in England to attend an important event. It was nerve racking, to say the least.

I also had to advise my employer, Mr. Anderson, of my decision and ask to reschedule my vacation of two weeks to the month of September. It was very unusual to be taking a vacation in September in England, and therefore he was understandably concerned about the proper oversight of the department in my absence.

I assured him that my assistant would be well guided for the occasion and having finalized the arrangement, it was now time to inform the party in Jamaica that I would be the UK delegate to their conference that year.

My close friend, Eddie Levy, decided that it would be a good idea and an opportune time for him to visit his parents. We booked our flight to Jamaica together on an American airline named National Airlines. The route involved a stop in Miami where we'd catch a connecting flight on Air Jamaica to Kingston. There was no direct flight from England to Jamaica at that time.

The prospects of seeing my relatives and friends back home caused a rippling excitement, despite the fact that my adopted parents who grew me from the age of three months had passed. It was my intention to make contact with my biological parents on arrival.

At last our departure date arrived and this September seemed different from all other Septembers as we journeyed to Heathrow Airport. This was my first time ever travelling by plane. Going through immigration was a great experience with the different check points involved, and then it was time to set foot on the plane. It was my first close up of any plane ever and I thought it was quite huge.

Then, as soon as my feet touched the steps to enter, I became nervous and began to sweat. By the time I got to my seat, my clothes were all wet. It was if a shower of rain had fallen on me between the steps and the entrance. The air hostess, perhaps recognizing my condition, assisted me by even fastening my seatbelt for take-off. As the plane sped down the runway my hands firmly gripped the most solid part of the seat, while I silently communicated with the Lord, as the aircraft lifted off the ground.

A few minutes in the air, I felt the urge to use the toilet and quickly unlocked the seatbelt and headed towards the sign indicating "Toilet," which was located behind my seat. As I began to walk briskly down the passageway, I immediately heard a shout from the air hostess saying, "Please sir, get back to your seat. We are still climbing." To add to my discomfort, I was now frightened and embarrassed with all eyes focused on me. I hurriedly returned to my seat and resumed praying, this time to hold my intended disposals until the earliest convenient time, which, thank God I did.

After some time, the pilot announced that we were now at 30 odd thousand feet and the seatbelt signs were now off. As for me, all was well. At this point, I felt a little relaxed and hoped for smooth flying all the way, while I made my way to the toilet.

On the serving of the meal, when asked what I wanted to drink, I requested a whiskey, which gave me the boost to endure the rest of the flight. I was told that the take-off and landing of the aircraft were the two periods of concern, therefore on landing in Miami, I went through a routine similar to the one in London, only this time I did not sweat.

The flight to Jamaica had its own moments of concern including my realizing that the aircraft was much smaller than previous one and was packed to capacity. I wondered if we would make it home, but thankfully, we did.

Finally, Eddie and I were in Jamaica after all these years, having left as boys we now returned as responsible adults. To be there to attend such an important event on behalf of so many Jamaicans was a wonderful feeling. But before that, there were some family matters to attend to. We headed directly to St. Elizabeth, where my first stop was in Santa Cruz to overnight with my biological father, Levan Clarke, who met me at the airport. Despite the long flight, most of the night was spent getting to know each other.

The following day, I went to Potsdam District where Munro College is situated and where I grew up till my 18th birthday. It was a pleasure to meet the older folks in the community, who expressed their delight in seeing me again and reminisced about my boyhood days among them, most of which were glowing.

After spending a few days at Munro, which everyone preferred to call 'Postom,' it was back to Santa Cruz and then off to Kingston to attend the PNP Conference at the National Arena.

I arrived for the public session of the conference on the third Sunday in September, and was given a great reception, during which I was introduced to the leaders of the party, such as Comrade Howard Cooke; Leacroft Robinson; Dudley Thompson, general secretary; Ken Chin Onn; Carlyle Dunkley, president of the National Workers Union, to name a few. Introductions were made by the party leader, Michael Manley with whom, by then, I shared a very close friendship.

It was indeed an exciting experience to be in the arena, which was packed with delegates and supporters. The general secretary informed me that I was expected to bring greetings from England to the gathering. I had every confidence I could do that.

While sitting on the platform, I began to make some jottings for my intended speech. Anticipating that by the time the other speakers had delivered theirs, I would be ready and would have observed the mood of the crowd. My expectations and excitement suddenly changed to surprise and nervousness, when after the Reverend Phillip Hart completed the devotion, I was called upon to bring greetings. I silently said, "Oh no! Not the first speaker," and then cold sweat washed over me. Walking up to the podium, my legs were like putty and then I remembered the words of my friend Cecil Collier, who sat beside me on the platform. "Don't worry, you are up to the task." I spoke for about 10 minutes, after which I got a standing ovation. I then felt ten feet tall. I also felt that the people in England in the PNP were now fully appreciated by the party at home.

The next day, which was Monday, I felt very honoured to be invited to have lunch with the prime minister and other senior members of the party at Jamaica House. That was another great experience.

On Tuesday, I had lunch with Mr. Carlyle Dunkley, the president and island supervisor of the National Workers Union, in what I thought was an interview. It led to a proposal to join the staff at the National Workers Union,

116

which I promised to give some consideration on my return to London. By all accounts, my trip to Jamaica was rewarding and fruitful. My journey back to London was as terrifying as the ride to Jamaica, with a lot of turbulence. I was overjoyed when the plane landed smoothly at Heathrow Airport.

I returned to work to a surprise welcome back from the boss, Mr. Anderson, who was curious to know all about Jamaica and my trip. The rest of the staff was pleasantly surprised when they heard of his approach, knowing that he never engaged black employees in conversation, but evidently considered that this was an exceptional moment.

Shortly after returning to London, the Labour Party announced the start of the campaign for the next general election, which was due in 1974. As secretary of the Trades Council, I had to be a part of the planning and coordinating committee, which comprised Trade Unions, Labour Party members of parliament, councillors and other members of all constituencies within the borough of Brent. I recall that my family was practically without a patriarch during this period of campaigning. The date of the election was finally set for February 1974 and the Labour Party was expected to do well as the campaign intensified.

THE MOST UNUSUAL
TURN OF EVENTS

Having carried out a vigorous campaign, the result of the February election was not to our liking, in that, no party had gained the majority of seats. The incumbent Conservative party led by Edward Heath, won the popular votes, but the Labour Party took a plurality of seats. Edward Heath as prime minister, tried to form a coalition with the Liberal party but failed. After that, Harold Wilson formed a minority government and took office in March 1974. We were glad to be in charge of the government once again, but realized that governing would be an uphill task. However, I was happy that the election was finally behind us and gradually settled down to normal duties, both at the workplace and Trades Council, in particular.

During the campaign period, we were alerted to the growing concerns of worker abuse by the management of a company named Grundig, which was located in the Willesden area, very close to the Trades Council's office. These workers were mostly of Asian origin and were struggling to get union representation and hence had made contact with the Council. I had hoped that after the election, my activities would lessen, which would give me time to spend with my family, but this was not to be.

I immediately started discussions with the unfortunate workers on issues relating to their conditions of employment and other concerns which they raised with the trade union leaders to see how we could best assist them in their plight. Unfortunately, before I could give my full attention to these workers, I received a call from the Jamaican High Commission in the second week of April, stating that Mr. Manley, now the prime minister of Jamaica, would be arriving in London for a few days and wanted to meet with me at his office. I wondered then, "How am I going to manage?" but decided then that I should never disappoint Mr. Manley as it must have been of some importance why he wished to meet with me.

On his arrival, the prime minister stated that he was on his way to France to attend the funeral of Georges Pompidou, the late president, who had died on April 5. Once he returned to London, he would to spend a few days meeting with as many Jamaicans as possible.

The high commissioner, had by then, made arrangements for him to visit Birmingham immediately to meet with Jamaican nationals in that area on his return to England. This was scheduled to take place at Ashton University, Birmingham. I was further advised by Mr. Laurel Bruce, the prime minister's personal assistant, that I was to accompany Mr. Manley on the trip to Birmingham. I hurriedly arranged with Comrade Aubrey Brown, the secretary of the Brent PNP group, to travel by car to Birmingham. On the appointed day, he took membership applications to the PNP UK and seized the opportunity to form a group in that city.

That day, I met with Mr. Manley's party at Euston Railway Station for the travel to Birmingham, and there to my surprise was a large number of Scotland Yard policemen and women and other Secret Service officers. I was thoroughly checked and verified before entering the coach, feeling a special sense of importance as we journeyed along.

On our arrival in Birmingham, the prime minister was whisked out of the compartment in such a hurry, that before I knew it, I was left alone at the station's platform and not knowing where we were going, I decided to proceed to Ashton University where the meeting was to be held. It took me a while to walk to the university, but on my arrival, I saw a police officer, and remembered the advice of my mother years ago, "If you are in doubt, ask a policeman."

I went to the policeman and explained my position and what had occurred. He smiled and said that the prime minister was taken to a hotel for refreshments and rest before attending the meeting. I was very impressed that the information was circulated to policemen throughout the city on the arrival of Mr. Manley.

Fortunately, a taxi was passing by just at that time, and the officer stopped the taxi and gave him the name and address of the hotel to which he should take me. At the hotel, Mr. Bruce and others who were of the view that I had gotten lost or gone back to London, enquired of my whereabouts. After a brief explanation, I too settled down for some refreshments and rest.

Mr. Manley's party arrived at the university at 6 pm to a jam packed gathering of Jamaican nationals and some other West Indians, who greeted him with loud cheers of welcome. Mr. Cecil Collier from the Jamaican High Commission, chaired the meeting and introduced the prime minister who spoke on many issues affecting Jamaica including education and the economy. He also mentioned the possibility of setting up a branch or branches of the Workers Bank in England to facilitate direct lodgements and other transactions to Jamaica, similar to that of The Bank of India, in England.

At the time for questions, I suggested to Comrade Aubrey Brown that because we did not know anyone at the meeting from Birmingham, the question should be asked by him as to how they, in that part of the country could join or become involved in the affairs of the People's National Party, which he did.

The question was like music to Mr. Manley's ears, and he quickly stated that the national organizer of the PNP groups, Comrade *Neville* Clarke was there with him and immediately called on me to address the question. After explaining our recruitment programme, Comrade Brown and I handed out the membership forms, which were completed and returned immediately with membership fees. In just one evening, the Birmingham group became a reality. It also became the largest of our groups in England. I made arrangements that night to return the following weekend for election of officers and to provide them with the party's constitutions, aims and objectives. That was a wonderful evening indeed.

As promised, the next weekend comrades Aubrey Brown, Winchester James, Charlie Graham and I returned to Birmingham to a proper welcome by our newly recruited members. We met at a night club where a large group of Jamaicans gathered to meet with us. Chief among them were comrades Bachelor, Buchannan, Cunningham and Sankey, who appeared at the time to be the most popular members with the black population in Birmingham. Together they proposed to hold an election for offices after sensitizing the large body of new members of the principles and objectives of the UK groups, which was outlined to them by me. A few weeks later, I received by mail the names and positions of the executive body of the Birmingham group, which was officially relayed to the party in Jamaica.

In the month of June that year, I received a letter from Mr. Carlyle Dunkley of the National Workers Union in Jamaica, formerly offering me a job in the union, which was not unexpected, considering the lengthy discussions we had during my visit to Jamaica. I had, on my return from Jamaica, discussed with my wife the possibility of an offer to work in Jamaica. But when the offer came, we deliberated long and hard before arriving at a decision, whether to accept or not.

These deliberations continued on and off over the next few weeks to determine whether or not I was about to do the right thing.

In July of 1974, which was shortly after officially concluding the formation of the Birmingham group, I received a telephone call from a Mr. Anthony Spalding, Minister of Housing and Works in Jamaica. He invited me to meet with him at the Park View Hotel in London, where he was staying. Although it was a busy time of year for me, I accepted the invitation readily. I had met him briefly in Jamaica the year before and remembered he was a very popular figure in Jamaica and in particular, Trench Town. I looked forward to meeting with him, so despite my full schedule, I arranged to meet the day after the call.

On arrival, he greeted me as if he had known me for a very long time and quickly offered me a drink of good 'ole Jamaican White Rum, which I very rarely consumed, but could not resist on that occasion. We sat across from each other as he proceeded to outline the reason for the meeting, recognizing as he did, my role in the PNP and other involvement in the communities in London. He sought my assistance in a fundraising exercise for the building of a sports complex in Trench Town, Jamaica, which was part of his constituency. Part of my role was to invite as many Jamaicans as I could to a meeting at the Jamaican High Commission office a couple of days later. I accepted with pleasure.

The meeting, which was chaired by Dr. Arthur Wint, the high commissioner, was well attended and included notable persons such as Dudley Thompson, the Minister of Foreign Affairs in Jamaica and Mr. Jeremy Thorpe, the leader of the British Liberal Party. Minister Thompson was presented to the audience by Dr. Wint. He was en route to Jamaica from Africa when his close friend Minister Spalding asked him to stop in at the meeting. After some brief comments on the situation in Jamaica and his trip to Africa, Minister Thompson introduced the member of parliament for South East St. Andrew, Comrade Anthony Spalding. He also asked the audience for their full support of Mr. Spalding. At the end of the minister's presentation, many persons donated cash, while others made pledges to the project. From all appearances, the event was a rewarding one for the Trench Town complex and community.

The months of July and August were very challenging. I had by then decided to accept the job with the National Workers' Union in Jamaica. I would go there alone for a self-imposed six month probationary period. If things went well, the family would join me, if not, I'd return to England. With the plan in place, preparations for my family's sustenance in England during my absence, took priority over all other activities. Funds had to be secured to meet their expenditure for at least six months and I needed money for airfare plus an additional sum to sustain me in Jamaica for six months just in case things did not proceed as expected from the get go.

It didn't help my situation one bit that during the weeks leading up to the end of September 1974, the Harold Wilson led government was experiencing difficulty in ruling as a minority government and took the decision to call another general election in October. This was just eight short months after the last, so despite my personal plans, as I was still the secretary of the Trades Council and a senior member of the Labour Party locally, I was forced back on the campaign trail.

The October election resulted in a narrow victory with a majority of three seats for the Labour Party, thus giving them a better opportunity to govern. I was delighted that this was all over and with some measure of success. I was now free, I hoped, to continue my preparations for departure, which was to be at the end of February 1975.

THE BOMBSHELL

ometime in the month of November, I attended a meeting of the Brent Accident Prevention Council at the Brent Town hall. After the adjournment, Alderman Phillip Hartley invited me into his office for a chat. Now that the election was behind us he wanted to let me know that Mr. Laurie Pavitt, who was the member of parliament in the constituency that I lived, had indicated that he might not complete the full term of office this time around. The Labour Party leadership in the constituency had considered me the most suitable person to succeed him, if and when the time came, particularly because of my position in the borough.

I was flattered by his comments and wondered why now? Why at this time when I have already made my decision to go to Jamaica? I calmly explained the decision that my family and I had made regarding going back to Jamaica. My friend, Alderman, like my other colleagues in the Trades Council to whom I announced the news the following week were shocked to hear that I intended to relinquish such a powerful position and the prospects I had of even greater prominence, to return to Jamaica after all these years. My friend, Ken Spence, of the Trades Council was devastated by the sudden news and accused me of not being a true friend since I withheld such an important decision from him.

My next task was to advise my employer, Mr. Anderson, with whom I had become very close and then the PNP UK group members from London to Birmingham, who had accepted me as their local leader. I would then advise all other boards and organizations on which I served.

The series of announcements became very daunting and had me wondering if I had made the right decision. After 20 years of hard work in England I now faced the awesome prospect of becoming the first black member of parliament in the history of England, and instead I chose to leave that and my family and friends behind. Oh, I wondered and pondered and then finally remembered the vision upon leaving Jamaica: to learn, earn and return.

In the month of December, the struggle for union representation by the workers at the Grundig factory had intensified. There were several meetings with the workers but attempts to have dialogue with the management was impossible. I was unhappy that in my final days as secretary of the Trades Council, I could not resolve the matter successfully and the dispute was therefore passed to my successor to continue the fight.

Christmas of 1974, was not much of a merry one for us because of my impending departure. For some unknown reason, the children seemed excited at the thought of me going to Jamaica and the possibility of them going to live there one day and suddenly all my friends appeared to want to go to Jamaica as well. This encouraged me and made me very hopeful.

My last meeting with the Brent Trades Council on the 25th of February, 1975 was more of a farewell event, punctuated only by the election of a new general secretary. My successor was my very good friend, Jack Dromey, who later in life became the deputy general secretary of the Transport and General Workers Union, under the leadership of Jamaican born, Bill Morris. Later, he would marry another good friend of ours, Harriet Harmon, the former deputy prime minister under Gordon Brown.

It was now time to say fun farewell to most of my friends. Jeffery Palmer, the proprietor of the London Apollo Club, which was situated on the building owned by the Trades Council, had decided early in January to host a send-off party for me. It was scheduled for the 27th of February, two days before my departure.

Among the many guests who attended were Dr. Arthur Wint, Jamaican high commissioner; Alderman Phillip Hartley; Mr. Reg Freeson, minister of housing; Mr. Laurie Pavitt, member of parliament for the constituency, Kenny Spence, chairman of the Brent Trades Council; Jack Dromey, new general secretary of the Trades Council, members of the PNP groups from Tooting, Hackney, Brent and Birmingham. It goes without saying that family members represented well including, the Pennycooks of course, the Necktie Gang, Rocky Pennycook, Darrel Blackwood, better known as 'Doctor', Dudley McBean, Edward Levy and a host of other friends that I had met along the way. It was an evening of splendour and mixed emotions, highlighted with the performance of a Turkish belly dancer. A number of guests brought tributes expressing their pleasure in our relationship, but surprisingly it was Phillip Hartley's comments which brought shock to the gathering, when he said, and I quote: "I will miss my friend and hope that when he goes to Jamaica, he fails, so that he can come back to us, but knowing him as I do, he will never fail."

When I heard those words, tears flowed down my cheeks, I was overcome by the sentiments expressed by all speakers, so much so, that my response could be described as the shortest in British history. It was the end of an era, spanning twenty years of a sentimental journey from the Windrush Generation that will be remembered for many years to come as a result of this book.

Two days later, I hugged and kissed my family goodbye and headed back to Jamaica.